SHOP SOCIAL

SHOP

CONNECT WITH THE PEOPLE + PRODUCTS THAT SUPPORT YOUR BEST LIFE

SOCIAL

DANA ROEFER

LIONCREST
PUBLISHING

SHOP SOCIAL

Connect with the People + Products that Support Your Best Life

ISBN 978-1-5445-3121-2 *Hardcover*

978-1-5445-3120-5 *Paperback*

978-1-5445-3119-9 *Ebook*

978-1-5445-3230-1 *Audiobook*

For my friends, my "circle,"

Kelli, Lauren, Lisa, Nicole, Denise, Jennifer,

Valerie, Charleigh, Katie, Anna, and Chelsea, whom

I have the pleasure of purchasing from regularly,

for keeping me at my very best.

And for the other 7.7 million[1] sellers

throughout America who are dreaming of a new life

and freedom for their family (and are achieving it!)

while simultaneously helping others

reach their goals.

You are my inspiration

and I'll always be your greatest

cheerleader and advocate.

---

[1] Direct Selling Association, "Industry Fact Sheets," 2022 https://www.dsa.org/statistics-insights/factsheets

Contents

Introduction

We're tired.

Tired of all the noise from the news media, from social media, from everyone who doesn't know us, yet they all have an opinion about who we're supposed to be. They tell us what we should look like, what we should want, and what we all need.

So. Much. Noise. It's exhausting.

We're surrounded by remarkable women who don't recognize how amazing they are. How could they, when they—*we*—are constantly being told we should want something else, that we need something else, should *be someone else*?

We're busy. We have enough on our plates without having to live up to all these expectations. Why should we? Still, that perfect woman in our heads, the one we're supposed to be, reminds us every day: *You are not doing enough.*

It's demoralizing. We and so many of our highly motivated, hard-driving friends are doing so much with our lives—as friends, moms, wives, and working professionals—yet we feel like failures. Not complete failures. But like we're failing every day with the little things. The things that could make the difference between getting by and mastering our lives. Between being almost good enough and great.

We believe our bodies are not what they should be. Our parenting, too, is lacking. Our marriages, our careers—our *lives*—do not meet today's standards of success.

We have unrealistic *personal* expectations, often driven by unrealistic *societal* expectations. We want to do more and do better, but we're afraid that whatever we do will be the wrong next step. I witness women struggling with these challenges on a daily basis, and it hits so close to home. It is my story too.

I remember living through those times. Day after day, I felt like I was surviving, but not thriving. I knew there was more to life—more opportunity for so many things that mattered, truly *mattered* to me. I wanted to feel better. I wanted to be better. I wanted to show up better. I wanted so much.

At the same time, I was being told I should want those things, but I should want these other things too. I should want it all and have it all. What was "all," exactly, and how do I get it? Because the "all" the world was showing me didn't match *my* "all"—at all—and frankly, I wasn't even sure what my all was!

I needed clarity. I needed to figure out what really mattered to me. What would make me happy, fulfilled? What would make my life complete? And I needed to know how to get it.

MY JOURNEY AND YOURS

Let's get one thing straight: You are amazing. You're an incredible woman. Wherever you are right now is exactly where you should be in your story, your lifelong journey, your pursuit of whatever makes you happy.

When I started my own journey, I was where I needed to be too (even though I didn't realize it at the time). I just had to get clarity on what I wanted and who I wanted to be. From there, it was a matter of trusting myself to make the best choices for me. I am still on that journey, and in this book, I hope you will join me on your own journey too. We'll both have setbacks, but they will make the progress that much more rewarding. We'll have good days and challenging days too, but the toughest days make the good ones that much better. We don't have to do it all today, this week, or even this year. There's no deadline for joy, peace, and fulfillment. You will get there when you get there.

So take a deep breath. Let go of all the expectations others have put on you—your family, your friends, your neighbors, and especially the strangers that surround us on social media and in society in general. Let go of the expectations you put on yourself—let's be honest, those can be much worse than the others! Let's start from a new place, a new reality.

In this new reality, we get real about who we are and what we want. But we don't stop there. We take the next step: we pursue what we want by being more intentional about our actions—specifically, about how we allocate our resources.

Consider your resources—your time and money—and how you spend them. Yes, I'm talking about your buying habits. We spend a lot of energy deciding what to buy and where to buy it. And frankly, much of that time, money, and energy is wasted because so often we don't get what we want or need.

What does shopping have to do with everything I've talked about so far? Think about it: Shopping is how we bring things into our lives—products, services, experiences. Collectively, these things can improve our lives. Too often, they let us down. Because the traditional way of shopping is hard and often unsuccessful.

I'll let you in on a little secret: *I hate shopping.* Ironic, right? Especially since this book is *about* shopping. So I found a new way to shop, one that removes all the barriers, all the worry, and all the negatives around shopping and turns it into a completely different experience. No more endless choices with no way to figure out which is the *best* choice. No more buying from people I don't know and companies I don't trust. No more collecting piles of makeup that aren't the right color, clothes that don't quite fit, and household products that make my family sick. No more wasting time shopping for the wrong things.

Here's my other secret: I love *social* shopping. Unlike traditional shopping, it allows me to use my time efficiently to get exactly what I want. I discovered it many years ago—grew up with it, in fact—but it wasn't until I was an adult, a mom, and a wife, trying to run a household that I realized just how much shopping social could change my life. And I discovered armies of women out there willing to help me.

Through my own journey and those of other women, I've recognized common threads we all follow to go from merely surviving to full-on thriving. In this book, I'll take you through those threads with stories and lessons gleaned from my own experiences and those of other women. We'll start with intentionality because change requires making decisions about our lives and then taking intentional actions to satisfy those decisions. Then we'll talk about who you are and what you want in this life for yourself, your home, and your family. We'll discuss how to get it through shopping social. I'll address all the negatives that are swimming around in your head too. In fact, I have a whole chapter about that! Because I know you're smart, realistic, and you want all the facts. I'll also tell you how to get real results from shopping social, because I don't want to waste your time. Finally,

I'll show you how shopping social isn't only a solution for yourself; it's also a way to support your friends, those women entrepreneurs who genuinely care about you, and whose lives have been changed through shopping social.

FROM CONSUMER TO INVESTOR: THE MINDSET SHIFT

Shifting my buying habits from being a traditional shopper to becoming a social shopper didn't happen for me right away. It didn't happen overnight either. For years, I was simply a consumer.

Wait, you're thinking, *Aren't you still a consumer? Aren't we all consumers?*

Yes, in a way. Companies produce goods and services, and we consume them. I consume them. The shift I'm talking about is how I chose to allocate my resources to acquire those goods and services. I could *consume* whatever was out there, or I could make *intentional investments* in my family, my home, and myself—investments that improved our lives with goods and services that made the time, money, and effort I devoted to acquiring them worth the trade.

In simpler terms, I had to get clarity on the outcomes I was seeking. I had to acknowledge those outcomes were important to me—that the health and happiness of my family and me, and having a healthy, organized, peaceful home environment were top priorities. And I had to commit to achieving those outcomes with the best solutions. Often, those solutions came in the form of products.

But here's the thing, and this is critically important, so I want to be as clear as possible: This shift, at its core, had nothing to do with money, or buying, or shopping. The mental shift was deciding that my family, my home, and I deserved the best. We deserved to be healthy, joyful, and fulfilled. We deserved to have things that made our lives easier and better.

Once I shifted my mindset to acknowledge this fact, the solution was obvious. I could continue to accept life as a consumer, or I could choose to change direction and become an investor in my family, home, and self. I chose this new direction and became an investor.

As I began intentionally deciding what I needed, I also looked for the right people to assist me in each area of my life. Who could I trust for advice on my health, on my home environment, and with specialized topics like skincare? In this way, I built a sort of micro-community of expert women—my social sellers or "circle" as I came to refer to them.

At first, I thought social shopping would be hard. I worried it would be expensive too. In fact, the opposite was true. Once I had clarity around what I wanted, my circle did most of the work for me. They asked me what problem I was trying to solve, and based on their expertise, they recommended the best products, programs, and routines for my needs. They made shopping fast and efficient, and they found me great deals! This gave me time for other activities—like spending even more time with my family and my husband, going on a hike or to yoga, and reading to my kids.

Sometimes the individual products seemed to cost a little more compared to big-box store prices, but they were on par with department store prices. Over time, the cost was actually less, though, because they were exactly what I needed. I wasn't collecting products that didn't quite work—you know, all those personal and household products that sit in a closet or take up drawer space because you never use them, but you can't bring yourself to throw them away either. Instead, I was getting products that worked for me better than anything I'd ever used before. Often, I had to use less of them, or use them less frequently because they worked so well.

If my social seller's product didn't quite hit the mark, I could return it. We would discuss what didn't work. Then she could use that information to find something better for my needs. It was like having my own personal shopper. She wasn't trying to sell me anything—she was trying to solve my problems.

I say "she," but over time, I've met many social sellers and I count on them for a variety of solutions. I trust them to find the best products for what I need. They don't see me as a consumer. They know I'm an investor, and they want to help me make the best choices for the highest return on my investments.

Interacting with my circle and talking among my friends about the products, I discovered I wasn't alone. Other women were engaged in shopping social as an efficient, effective method for achieving their goals. Like me, they were becoming the best versions of themselves through shopping social.

This isn't about using better products. It isn't really even about shopping. While those actions are a big part of the solution, the real goal here is self-acceptance and appreciation. It's about learning who you are and embracing yourself with all your beauty, your strengths, and your weaknesses too. It's about giving yourself permission to shift your expectations from what you think they should be, ones you've been told they should be, to expectations and desired outcomes that actually matter—truly *matter*—to you and no one else. Because trying to make everyone happy is ridiculous and guaranteed to make you miserable. Learning to accept and appreciate yourself, on the other hand, is within your grasp. It's within all of us.

When I say accept and appreciate yourself, I'm talking about you in this moment. Not the future you who's lost twenty pounds. Not the future you who's the perfect mom, the ideal spouse, the best friend to all, and the life of the party. (Trust me, no one is all those things.) You are amazing right now. Start from there. Embrace who you are. Then examine your expectations. Throw out the ones that don't matter and zero in on the ones that do. Visualize the outcomes you desire. All of that has to happen first. Then and only then, look to shopping social to take you to the next step, where you invest in yourself for a better life.

My journey from consumer to investor wasn't without challenges. I struggled to figure out who I was and what I wanted. Putting into words what I wanted for myself, my home, and my family wasn't as easy as it sounds. Taking those desired outcomes to my circle of social sellers, discussing them with these women, wasn't easy either. I felt vulnerable, as if I were letting them into the most intimate corners of my life. Did I want to tell someone how I wanted my hair to look, my skin to feel? Did I want to confide in another woman that I had no idea what the best colors were for my complexion, the best clothing styles for my body type? Not at first. But the more I reached out, the more I realized how much they wanted to help. They cared. They wanted me to achieve my goals. They seemed as invested in the process as I was. And they were experts!

Okay, maybe not all of them. In every industry there are experts, there are people who are still learning, and unfortunately, there are those who don't have a clue. I sorted this out pretty quickly, though, and identified those women I could count on to get me from the "me" I loved then to the future "me" I might love even more...with a little help.

I also learned that getting what I wanted demanded a certain commitment from me. There is no such thing as a miracle cure, and I had to commit to a product and allow it the time necessary to work.

Change doesn't happen overnight, but in time, the incremental differences you see by using a better supplement, a better shampoo, a better hand cream, are evident.

HOW I GOT HERE

My mom has always been particular about self-care. She got shopping social before shopping social was cool. In hindsight, I don't know why it took me so long to figure it out, but I'm glad I did.

When I was a kid, I'd pick up products like laundry detergent for my mom from a product bin on a neighbor's porch. I'd visit another neighbor, and they'd go to their product closet to grab something else, like shampoo, that Mom had ordered. I remember swimming in our backyard pool one day, as my mom and her friends gathered around doing color analyses for each other. By matching their skin tone and hair to color swatches from a kit, they were learning whether they were a "spring," a "summer," a "fall," or a "winter," and how this information could help them choose the most complimentary makeup and clothing for their particular coloring.

These were the old days of social shopping, and in a way, nothing has changed. Like Mom, I'm buying from people I know. I'm getting guidance from people who know more about personal and household products than I do. I'll have much more to share about this, and why I'm such a huge fan of shopping social, in the coming chapters.

But a lot *has* changed too. I remember my dad scoffing at the whole idea of shopping social. We didn't call it shopping social back then —it was called direct selling, multi-level marketing, and a lot of other things. In some circles, it had a very bad reputation, and for good reason. There were sellers who didn't take the time to understand their customers, or even the products they were selling. They focused so much on the business opportunity that they tended to forget the fact that they were dealing with people. I heard my dad's skepticism and saw that it wasn't without warrant. I also saw my mother achieve her goals by working with the *right* people. These were women she knew and trusted. Some were friends, while others were women she had been referred to by her friends.

I grew up, of course, got married and had children. I also fell into the typical habits of the average consumer, buying products off the shelf. I was often disappointed, but this seemed to be how people shopped. Buy something, hoping it worked. I hadn't even figured out what I wanted it to do beyond a vague desire (make my hair look better, for example), and all I had to rely on for an expected outcome was the promise on the label.

I'm naturally curious. I've always been a problem solver and a growth junkie. Like many of you, I'm always striving to learn more, do more, and have a better life. I wanted to help myself and my family. This was my responsibility, right? Yet the products I chose to improve our lives seldom lived up to my expectations.

I started asking questions of my own friends, just as I saw my mom doing when I was a kid. I wanted to learn what was working for them. Seeing their successes and learning their stories sparked memories of growing up in my mom's circle of friends, the man with the bin on his porch, the other woman with a closet full of goodies.

I dove back into shopping social to see if it was for me, and the results were much more than I had hoped for.

Full disclosure: I am not a social seller. I'm a woman who's been married for thirteen years. I have a wonderful husband and two darling young boys. And throughout my professional career, I've worked with a variety of entrepreneurs—many of them women—at various stages in their businesses. Many of these new companies were startups where the entrepreneur had to create their own product or service, build their own business structure, and do everything else that comes with starting and running a business. I got an up-close and personal look at how difficult these startups were to manage, especially compared with social selling.

Today, I'm a corporate consultant, a LifePlan facilitator, and a woman who has figured out who I am, what I want, and how to get it. Beyond helping myself and my family, I'm always looking for ways to help other women who are exactly where I was: treading water, doing their best to be moms and wives, plus running a household and working—or in the case of those entrepreneurs, running their own businesses—but always feeling as if they're falling a little bit short. I wanted to help these women, and I realized that through shopping social, I could help them while helping myself.

First, in order to initiate my own changes, I had to acknowledge who I truly was and decide who I wanted to become. I had to prioritize that woman's wants and needs. The changes I made were uncomfortable. I felt awkward and was tempted many times to slide back into my comfortable old rut of believing what I had always believed and doing what I had always done. But stagnating has never been my style. I had to grow. I had to do better. I'm still working on me, and I'm helping other women work on themselves too. I want them and I want you to find that peace and fulfillment you deserve.

We all need a circle: people who can help us reach our goals, find solutions to our problems, and give us what we need because they have the kind of expertise and access to products and services that we do not.

As you read this book, be on the lookout for people you can invite into your circle. Who among your friends and acquaintances might help you live your best life? You might have a friend who knows a lot about supplements—maybe they use them, or sell them, or both. It could be a casual acquaintance who dresses well and could give you advice on your own clothing or point you to a social seller who represents a brand you've never heard of that suits your style. People in your circle can even include a gym trainer, a life coach, or a therapist.

I'm not a therapist or a counselor. Like I said, I'm not even a social seller. I'm a woman who has been where many women are, where you may be, and I've seen what's possible when I opened my life up to solutions I hadn't considered. I won't tell you what to do, but I will show you what I did and what other women did and tell you about the outcomes. Then you can launch your own journey and find your own solutions.

We have choices in life. We don't have to settle. We don't have to be reactive. We can switch gears, become proactive, and create the lives we want, the lives we dream of. We can change our lives in dramatic and amazing ways. The sooner you discover this and act on it, the sooner you'll reap the rewards. But no matter how old you are, how long you've been married, or how many kids you have, it is never too late to make the shift. It's never too late to get what you want.

Let's go get it.

PART ONE

YOU ARE RESPONSIBLE FOR YOU

A beautiful life is closer than you think. If you spend your days wishing that if things were different, then you would be happier—stop wishing and start acting. Don't settle for a life that isn't fulfilling. It's never too late to look inward and start your journey. You have the power to become the person you want, to create the life you want. All it takes is getting clarity about what you want for yourself and the intentionality to make the choices necessary to make your vision a reality.

Because I committed myself to clarity and intentionality, I am happier and healthier today than I've ever been. I'm not going to sugarcoat it and say it was easy to get to this point, because it was the hardest thing I've ever done. Building my confidence and learning how to identify my needs and invest in myself took a long time. I went through many rough patches before I realized I have control and I don't have to be reactionary. The hardest part was letting myself be vulnerable and relying on others to help me get to where I am today.

You, and you alone, have the power to make real change in your life—but that doesn't mean you have to do it alone. There's a network of incredible women who want to help you become the best version of yourself. You can make real change in your life, but you need to first figure out who you are and what you need so you can connect with the right people and products to get you there.

It will take effort, resilience, and time, but you can get there. I'm proof. I promise you it's worth it. Looking back at how unhealthy and unhappy I was before I started my journey, I am forever grateful for the changes I've been able to make.

Let yourself dream. Let yourself be vulnerable. Let yourself act.

Give yourself permission to become the woman you've always wanted to be.

Chapter 1

INTENTIONALITY

Going into eighth grade, my life and friends revolved around sports. So when I failed my sports physical a few days shy of the fall season, I was devastated—and not only because I couldn't play. It was worse than that. The doctor said I had scoliosis. I'd never noticed the problem (nor had anyone else) because the two forty-five-degree-angle curves in my back making a backwards "s" were equal, hiding the curvature to me and the outside world.

As if that news weren't bad enough, I had to wear a back brace. What a way to start eighth grade! My social life was over before it had even started. Dramatic, I know. The brace wasn't noticeable under my clothes, but my self-conscious teen self was worried I'd be found out as "the girl with the problem," the girl who was different—who was *less than*. I'd head to the girl's bathroom the minute I got to school to take off the brace and stash it in my bag, then put it back on in the afternoon before going home so my mom wouldn't know.

Thankfully, after we figured out what was going on, I was still able to play basketball, volleyball, softball, and cheer the next handful of years. But despite regular sessions with a physical therapist and chiropractor, my scoliosis didn't get better. In fact, the sports activities made it worse. I kept playing anyway, through middle school and into high school. My spine suffered from the activity, and my sports performance suffered from my misaligned spine.

By my sophomore year, I had a decision to make. I could quit playing and stop injuring my spine, or I could get corrective surgery, which would likely also end my ability to play sports. However, it would improve my functionality and equalize my hips, increasing my chances of giving birth naturally in the future. I decided to get the surgery.

My orthopedic surgeon at the time was a fine physician, but something was lacking. She was tending to the scoliosis, but she wasn't taking care of me, Dana. In her eyes, I was a condition to be treated instead of a person to be healed. At least, that's how I felt, and it wasn't good enough. I wanted more than just enough functionality, just enough health.

I could have brushed off my concerns and trusted my spine to this professional, but I wanted a doctor who wanted what was best for me now and for the rest of my life. Even though I was just a teenager, I had to stand up for myself and find a new orthopedic surgeon. My parents were surprised when I gave them the news, but they could see how important this decision was to me. They agreed, and I fired my surgeon. We found a doctor I liked and trusted, one who saw me, the girl who wanted more from life than a straighter spine and acceptable health.

This was the first time in my life that I recognized I could be proactive instead of reactive. I could be intentional in creating my future instead of letting it happen to me. The spinal surgery went perfectly with no complications, and though I never played organized sports again, carrying and giving birth to my children was possible—a higher priority than sports had ever been!

I've carried this intentionality throughout my life, not just when it comes to medical decisions, but in all of my decisions, including how I invest my resources. My time is limited and precious, so what I do with it, and how I spend the money I earn with my time, matter. I'm intentional about what I do every day, and about the products I buy.

GETTING UNSTUCK WITH INTENTIONALITY

Stuck. Static. *Stagnant.* These are words that might describe your life right now. Don't feel bad—we all have seasons like that. From time to time, I still find myself feeling stuck, static, and even stagnant. Then I remind myself: Hey Dana, wake up! You have choices. You fired your orthopedic surgeon when you were a kid—surely you can make thoughtful decisions about the rest of your life. We all have choices to get what we want, even when getting what we want—or getting from where we are now to where we want to be—seems impossible. We can switch gears from reactive to proactive, but we must choose to create the life we want.

I'm sure you've heard the expression, "The best time to plant a tree is twenty years ago. The second-best time is now." It's time to plant that tree. Recognize your power and act on it. Right now, while it's fresh in your mind, write it on a sticky note and put it on your wall, your refrigerator, your bathroom mirror:

"I am not reactive. I am a proactive woman who makes intentional choices that serve my best interests, deliver what I want, and get me from where I am now to where I want to be."

You may need two stickies.

Too much? Yeah, I know. I've been there. It's a lot. Where you want to be may seem like a million miles away. Think of intentionality as a shortcut that makes things happen for you much more quickly than they ever have. Shifting from reactive to proactive makes those million miles a lot shorter.

Marcy

My friend Marcy worked at the same company for thirty years. She was miserable, but she stuck with the job. Marcy recited this mantra to herself, one you may be reciting to yourself about your job, your relationships, your life: *Just five (ten? fifteen?) more years, then I can do what I really want.* Five years doesn't seem like a long time, but when you're unhappy and dreaming about that other life you could be living, five years is an eternity.

When Marcy told me how unhappy she was in her job, I asked, "What if you did something different with these last five years?"

What if? It's a powerful question. "What if" inspires thoughts, dreams, opportunities for what's possible. What if you stepped through the "what if" doorway and executed your power of free will to make those what ifs realities? And what if you did it now instead of waiting five years?

I'm not suggesting you quit your job, sell your house, and move to Costa Rica (unless that's what you want, then by all means...). But what if, instead of waiting five years, you got real with yourself and took responsibility for your life right now—your life today and what it's going to look like in the future? Because no one else will do it for you. And really, we're not a bunch of princesses waiting around to be rescued, are we?

Marcy chose to work and live on her own terms and left the company. Now she's spending her last five years before retirement working for a ministry that makes her heart sing. She had no idea her work could be this fulfilling—gone are the days of dragging herself out of bed every morning. Marcy found her calling, and she loves her work at the ministry so much that she sees herself continuing it part-time in her retirement.

Intentionality is the secret power we have, but it takes practice. You don't have to stay in a job that makes you unhappy. In fact, you don't have to follow a traditional career path at all. The age-old checklist of school, college, marriage, homeownership, kids, and retirement might not be the right path for you. You have the freedom and the power to create your own path.

Do it for yourself and for everyone you care about. You'll be a better partner, friend, and mother when you're happy with your life instead of just going through the paces, following someone else's rule book. You'll also set a better example for your children and help them see that with intentionality, they too can choose a different path—a better path—in life.

Michael

It isn't just women who stick with the old "tried and true" path in life, or who unintentionally project those predictable roles onto our children. Attending an expo years ago, I chatted with a man at one of the booths. Michael had started his career on the corporate path, and over the years he had worked diligently from one promotion to the next until he found himself in the ranks of executive management. It was there at the pinnacle of his career that Michael realized he wanted more out of life. He made the courageous decision to walk away from the "golden handcuffs" to pursue his passion project—the restaurant.

Our conversation shifted to Michael's high-school-age son, Austin, and Michael's frustration that he wasn't interested in school. Michael felt that his son should be thinking ahead toward college and a career, but Austin wouldn't even go on campus tours. Michael worried about his son's future.

"So you want your son to get good grades, go to college, get a good job, and climb the corporate ladder, like you did," I said. "What happens in thirty years when he gets to where you were not so long ago and realizes he hates that life, just like you did?"

Michael was scripting a life for his son that he himself wouldn't repeat. Realizing this absurd contradiction, he agreed and thanked me for my objective insight. After many years following a traditional path that made him unhappy, Michael had found the courage to change careers. Yet this mindset he had followed most of his life was so powerful, so invasive, he had failed to see that he was setting his son up for the same unhappiness.

BREAKING FREE THROUGH SELF-DIRECTION

It can be hard to move off of the traditional path. Painful, even. So how can you break away? With *self-direction*. The problem is that many people don't know how to be self-directed. They've been following directions all their lives, so when the option of self-direction becomes available, they don't know what to do. They end up seeking someone else to show them the way, when "the way" isn't what someone else says. The way is within each individual, and it's within you.

This lack of self-direction was clearly evident during the recent pandemic, when work-from-home and remote learning were forced on people used to adhering to a schedule, working on site and in the office, and learning in the classroom. Self-directed people thrived. Many others struggled, unable to devise or follow a schedule. If you were one of these people who struggled, join the club. Many people have been taught to rely on others to make decisions for them from the time they grabbed a parent's hand to cross the street until much later in life, waiting for their boss to assign them tasks or their professor to assign them homework.

It's time for new work and a new education—work and learning that serves you, not someone else. You have choices. The best (and possibly worst) part about these choices is that no one else can make them: it's all on you. This freedom can be terrifying—but it's really as simple as knowing what you want.

Clarity

First, you need clarity around what you want. Take a good look at all aspects of your life and ask yourself where you are today and how you got here. Most likely, you made good decisions and bad ones that brought you to your current situation. It's okay if you don't love all of it—you have the rest of your life to make changes.

Think about what's important to you. What gets you up in the morning and through the week? Who are the people that make life worth living? Where are the places you love spending time, and what are the activities you can't wait to do?

Visualize what you want your life to be. Imagine your perfect day—where you are, who's with you, and what you are doing. How big is the gap between that perfect day and your life today?

If you can't visualize your perfect day, consider what's most important to you. What could you never, ever live without? And what is it that you do not have in your life, and want to have, or that you have too little of in your life and want more of?

Before leaving my corporate job, I thought I'd need to do a lot of soul-searching to identify what was important to me. But once I put pen to paper to figure it out, the answer was simple: I valued personal health, the health of my family, my relationship with my husband, and spending time with my children and other members of my family. The gap between those priorities and how I was spending my time and energy was a big one, and I knew I had to adjust and walk away from that role if I had any chance of turning the better life I visualized into a reality.

With those priorities in mind, I then turned to Tom Paterson's LifePlan process, described in the book *Living the Life You Were Meant to Live*,[2] to help me identify my needs.

You don't have to follow this same process to identify your needs, but it's simple and I recommend it. One of the tools within The LifePlan process uses four guiding questions to help you determine what is true in your life right now. Write these down in a notebook, an online document, or in an email to yourself. Then answer them:

1. **What's right?** These are all the things in your life that are good and that should be kept! You do not want to make changes that impact or take away from that which is good.

2. **What's wrong?** This is what you need to change.

3. **What's confused?** Confused items need clarity. Dig deep here.

4. **What's missing?** Think about how you can add this to your life.

---

[2] Tom Paterson, *Living the Life You Were Meant to Live* (Nashville: Thomas Nelson, 1998).

Identify what to keep, change, and add, and recognize those things that require more clarity. Then, use self-direction to make the intentional decisions that will deliver the life you really want. I do this exercise at least once a month and it is so helpful in keeping my goals on track.

If you're still unsure about what to do, don't worry—we're still in chapter 1. We have a lot more to talk about! But you may want to bookmark this page and come back to it whenever you have a decision to make and need clarity.

No matter what aspects of your life don't
reflect your ideals, you have the power to change them.
You can choose—and make reality—the life you want.
It all starts with getting clarity around what
you want and being intentional about
fulfilling these desires.

Back in high school, I decided my health was important. I decided that being able to bear children was important too, more important than playing sports. That moment of clarity drove me to make the critical decision to seek out a doctor who saw me and understood me, and to get the spinal surgery that helped me fulfill an important goal.

That clarity and intentionality were the beginning. I also had to learn to care about myself enough to make hard choices. Later, I had to care about my family enough to make difficult decisions too.

THIS ISN'T ABOUT BUYING PRODUCTS

This is a book about shopping social, but it's about much more than that. I won't encourage you to sign up for something you don't want or need. If I'm selling anything, it's selling you on the idea of you. Selling you on the idea that what you want in life is worth pursuing and believing in yourself enough to go get it. This book is an invitation for you to figure out what you need to be your best, your happiest, your most fulfilled. It's about making the connection between clarity and intentionality to live your best life.

1) What am I demanding of myself right now?

2) Are those demands reasonable? Do they bring me joy, peace, and happiness, or anxiety, fear, and dread?

3) What does my ideal life look like?

4) How big is the gap between my life right now and that ideal life?

5) What can I do today to begin closing that gap?

Chapter 2

KNOWING YOU,
GROWING
YOU

My friend Sara has a closet full of nearly identical black leggings. One day, she texted me to ask whether she should buy a pair of purple leggings like the ones I have. She said she liked mine, but she wasn't sure if she would be comfortable wearing anything but black.

Instead of texting Sara back, I called her.

"Why would you be uncomfortable wearing purple leggings?" I asked her, "Are you afraid to stand out?"

There was a pause. Then she replied, "Yes, I am. I feel like no one notices me in black leggings, and it's easier if I don't stand out."

Sound familiar? We all own too many black leggings, or sweat pants, or t-shirts. They help us blend in, so we don't have to worry about being noticed. We don't have to stand out. We also don't have to make a different decision than the one we've been making over and over again. Sara bought the same black leggings many times because it was the easy choice—the safe choice. Buying those leggings had become less of a choice and more of a habit. By the way, a habit is something you do without thinking. Without a clear motive. Without clarity or intentionality. Habits can be good—brushing your teeth, of course—but the wrong habits, or habits that don't fully support the life you want, can trap you in a place that doesn't allow for important, positive changes—the kind that close the gap between the life you have now and that other life you'd rather have. The one you have to identify, commit to, and sometimes fight for. That fight can begin with buying purple leggings, and it can blossom into an all-out battle for the truest, most confident version of yourself.

CONFIDENCE

Confidence comes from knowing who you are *and* putting that person out into the world. Sometimes it means abandoning the person you were and embracing who you are now or who you want to become. It doesn't matter how many black leggings you have in your closet—today could be the day you embrace your purple legging self. Or your teal legging, pink legging, or polka dot legging life, whatever.

Whomever you've been and who you are now is not who you're destined to be. You can always try something new and change and grow.

Don't be afraid to show off your inside self on the outside. Not the woman who unconsciously fell into a black legging habit and decided it was safer and easier, but the confident woman who secretly loves purple leggings and isn't afraid to wear them.

BEING SEEN

I started wearing makeup in eighth grade. Like Sara and her black leggings, I kept buying the same makeup and applying it basically the same way for two decades. My clothing style didn't change much either—lots of plain, solid clothing that didn't stand out or make *me* stand out.

Looking back at how I presented myself, it's clear I was afraid to be seen. More importantly, I wasn't investing in myself to become my true self. I avoided my best me—hid that woman from the world, choosing instead to present a dull, blank version of myself. An invisible version who didn't have to deal with the attention and maybe the conflict that might arise from being noticed.

As women, we're expected to invest in our homes and our families. We encourage our children to try new things—new foods, new interests, new hobbies—while we settle for day-to-day maintenance with no real growth. Too often we neglect ourselves. We don't invest in *us*.

One day, when I was in my early twenties, I went to my friend Christina's house. Christina was a cosmetologist and an expert in skincare and makeup application, so I turned to her to learn about my skin and the right makeup for me. She helped me with a skin assessment, and then she did my makeup. Christina did a great job. The makeup was very natural, and I still looked like myself. If anything, I looked *more* like myself.

Even so, my thoughts spiraled into anxiety: *I hope nobody notices. But I look different. They're going to notice. They're going to say something. What am I going to say back?*

The makeup was a minor change, but I didn't want to go anywhere in public or risk seeing anyone I knew. This was the moment I began to realize that I was terrified to be seen. It's taken years—decades, even—of therapy and journaling and conversations and questions to figure out how I can accept myself in a way that I am also willing to be seen by others.

You might be where I was in my early twenties. You might say, "There's no way I'm changing. I'm so afraid." I get it. But awareness is the first place you have to start. My awareness started at Christina's house, and I've continued to be curious about how to engage with it over time. Don't be afraid.

If you had asked me back then if I felt worthy of a change, or deserving of self-betterment, I would have said yes. Yet, deep down, I don't believe I did. Like many women, I was caught up in the belief that I was never good enough—could never live up to the standards of beauty set by the media and society in general. No matter what people closest to us say about how wonderful we are, we find it difficult to accept and internalize their words.

One night, when I was putting my son to bed, I said to him, "I am so proud of you. I am so proud to be your mom, and I'm grateful you're my son."

He looked up at me and said, "Mom, sometimes I don't know what to say when you say these things. I don't know what to say back."

I told him he didn't have to respond. He just had to hear me and believe me. After I tucked him in and closed the door, I paused for a moment, realizing I didn't always know how to respond either when people told me what I meant to them.

I don't love my children because of what they do for me—I love them just because they're my children. I love them unconditionally. If I could love them just for being them, expecting nothing in return, why couldn't I love myself for being me? Don't I deserve unconditional love too? I had to work on believing in my own self-worth. I had to forget about all the self-imposed contingencies upon which that self-acceptance relied. I had to believe I deserved love for being me, just like my son deserves my love simply for being my son.

We are all worthy of self-acceptance and self-love. We are all gifts to this world, and we shouldn't hide ourselves. We don't have to settle for black leggings and eighth-grade makeup. We can be exactly who we are and accept and love ourselves, not in spite of who we are, but because of who we are.

The Truth about Me Right Now

Grab a notebook and a pen. I want you to make a list called "The Truth about Me Right Now." Go ahead, find that pen. I'll wait.

Okay, now make a list of ten truths about yourself, focusing on the positive qualities. Here are some examples:

1. I'm creative.

2. My children love me.

3. I'm a loyal friend.

4. My singing brings people joy.

5. I know how to tell a joke.

If negative thoughts pop into your head, write those down too. Then scribble over them. They represent your fears, insecurities, and lack of confidence. Don't embrace those negative thoughts, destroy them. Replace each one with an opposite quality. For example, if you wrote "I can't cook," scribble that out and write what you *can* cook: "My chocolate chip cookies are to die for." Or write something else you do well: "I'm a good listener."

Read your list. Read it out loud. What do you think of this person? Pretty great, right? Like a woman who deserves the best in life. Yeah, that's *you*.

Tuck your list into a drawer in your desk or nightstand and take a peek at it every day. I actually keep a note going on my phone. Add to it. Celebrate the greatness that is you, and use the list as a gentle reminder that you are worth every penny, every ounce of energy, and all the time you invest in yourself. You are worthy, you are wonderful, and you owe it to yourself to be seen.

SUPERHEROES AREN'T REAL

It was 2016 when I first thought I should probably talk to a professional. Someone had recommended therapy to me, but in my family, we did not do therapy. We did not do problems. We did not do openness. We had a lot of walls. This was the first time I tried to really tackle vulnerability. I read books about vulnerability—and when I say read, I actually mean I started them and then returned them to the library because I wasn't ready for them yet. I eventually worked my way up to reading them.

In 2016, when I started working on vulnerability, I didn't know how much would be necessary two years later, in 2018 when I journeyed through one of the hardest situations of my life. You see, my husband and I are passionate. We are dreamers. We are doers. We care deeply about people and want to serve our community. We had started our own entrepreneurial venture, a school for our boys and for our community. It was our calling and it was so fun. We were filled with hope, joy, and excitement for the future of our children and for the children of our community.

Despite my passion for the school, it turned out to be a much bigger and more difficult project than I had imagined. I was a wreck every year. I battled every day, trying to lead valiantly, to muster the strength to fight. But I was afraid I would be seen—that I would be known. So I stayed back and did not walk in my power or the truth of who I knew I could be. I was in a constant internal battle with not being good enough and not being able to control everything. I recognized that every day we had to make decisions, but we didn't necessarily know which ones to make. I wanted the best for my kids. I wanted the best for my community. I wanted the best for my family. Everything got really rocky in 2018 when I came to a psychological place that was scary. I was completely depleted, and in 2021, we left the school.

During that time, in one of these moments of crippling emotions, my oldest son, Simon, came to me and asked, "Mommy, what's wrong?"

I said, "Mommy's learning that she's not Superwoman."

In his six-year-old wisdom, he said, "Mommy, it's okay. No one is. Superheroes aren't real."

It was so beautiful because it was what I needed to hear at that moment. Those three years were so brutal, but so beautiful because of my growth. It's during our hardest times that we find out who we actually are and who we want to be.

I decided who I wanted to be in February of 2021 when my family was on vacation in Florida. Still in the midst of so much hardship and struggle with our venture, I decided that I would not be reactionary anymore. I would be proactive in my life. I would invest in myself because I matter, not because of what anyone else says but because I knew it to be true.

I sat on the balcony and wrote a note saying, "Now's the time. I refuse to hide anymore. I refuse to keep playing scared because when I was scared, I was taken advantage of and betrayed. It was painful. I did not make all the right decisions, but the result was worse than I deserved."

You've had scenarios like this before. No doubt we all do. But it's what we do after those situations when we recognize what we are capable of, when we recognize the worthiness, which comes to us from our creator, that we need to walk in. That's what matters. So be fearless.

If you find yourself in a difficult spot, talk to someone. It is not weakness. It's growth, and growth takes incredible strength.

A BETTER YOU, INSIDE AND OUT

Gaining the confidence and making the investment in yourself to get what you want and create the life you desire can be an internal journey that eventually shows up on the outside. I decided to choose health and a vibrant life. For me, it all started with routine. I realized I had so many friends who were doing well and growing in areas I needed to grow in. I desired to get into a good, consistent exercise routine, and I was ready for a daily supplement program and a consistent skincare regimen.

These changes gave me the confidence to try more new things in my life. People responded to the changes they saw in me, and that gave me more confidence. I valued myself more, and I also found it easier to value others. I wasn't worried about what other people thought of me. I was more at peace, more content. That feeling showed in how I treated others. I was kinder and more loving. I actually began to care more about other people. When your life is full, and you have all the love, you don't feel the need to keep it all to yourself. You want to share it. The great thing is that giving it away doesn't deplete it from your life. In fact, you get more.

Start Small

You don't need to make a dramatic change to start putting more of yourself out there. Pick one thing, one habit you'd like to develop or one thing you'd like to change. Like me, you might start with new supplements, exercise, or skincare. Or like Sara, leggings in a new color, or other clothing you've admired on others, but never tried yourself. You might try a new haircut or style, jewelry, or a new scent. It doesn't have to be expensive, but remember you're investing in yourself, and you are worthy of the investment. Make one small change and see if it impacts the way you feel.

Sometimes when you've been stuck in the past, being less than the woman you truly are, a simple change can make a monumental difference in your attitude. As you gain confidence, try more new things. If you don't get it right the first time, try again. There's no limit to how many small changes you can make until you find what works for you.

Small steps can build to create dramatic results, not only in your outward appearance but in how you see yourself. They change how you carry yourself in the world, and what you can do in it.

Be Fearless

If you're nervous or worried about what other people will think, here's a secret: most people don't notice other people—including you—as much as you think they do. Worrying about the opinions and judgments of others wastes energy and eats away at your confidence. Don't let that kind of thinking steal your joy.

While you're busy thinking about how everyone else sees you, they're doing the same and are too focused on themselves to notice you. The woman in line behind you at the grocery store isn't focused on your purple leggings—she's thinking about her new haircut. She won't notice you're wearing a different shade of lip gloss or bigger earrings, because she doesn't know what you looked like yesterday and has nothing to compare your new look to.

Repeat after me: *This is about me. It's not about anyone else—just me.*

People who do see you every day are more likely to notice a change. They might compliment you, and that could go a long way toward dissipating any fears you have. You'll find that being seen isn't as horrifying a thought. If someone reacts negatively to your change, that's fine too. Remember: *This is about me. It's not about anyone else.*

Your husband may not notice your new highlights (in fact, he probably won't). That doesn't matter. The bottom line is this isn't about your hair, makeup, clothes, or jewelry. It's about investing in yourself to be the woman you were created to be, the woman inside you who deserves to be seen. It's about the small steps you take to bring that woman out and enjoy the confidence she brings. That's you. That's your confidence and your light, and you deserve it.

Get Help

Getting clarity around who you are can be an ongoing process. Using intentionality to confidently share who you are with the world is also a process, and you may not know where to start. My advice is to get out of your head and out in the world. Go to a public place, an outdoor café for example, and watch other people as they walk by. Can you see who is hiding and who isn't afraid to be seen? What catches your eye that rings true to who you are? Is there a color or a style that speaks to you and says, "This is you—why aren't you wearing me?"

Sure, you can do this online too, but it's not as effective. Seeing other women and how they move about and interact with others in the real world will give you a clearer sense of what it might feel like to wear those leggings or rock that hairstyle.

Look to your friends too. Who among them strikes you as comfortable and confident in their own skin? They don't have to be the most fashionable, by the way. They are simply women who know who they are and aren't afraid to be seen. Ask them for guidance. Tell them you're working on yourself and looking for recommendations on exercises, products, and services to assist with your growth.

You can also look to women outside your circle of friends for guidance. Don't be afraid to ask another woman on the subway where she got that coat or where she gets her nails done. The woman you ask may be on her own transformational journey, and you may be the stranger who confirms her decision to buy that coat, wear that nail color. Not that it matters—because those choices are all about her. But it doesn't hurt to support other women in their journeys as we pursue our own.

If you are struggling with your self-esteem, making these changes may not be enough to gain the confidence you deserve. Talk to someone you trust and ask them how they see you. Your friends see things that you do not. They recognize your beauty, your kindness, and your intelligence. They may never say it, but there is a reason they're your friends. They value you. Ask them why and prepare to be pleasantly surprised.

Knowing yourself, understanding your worth, and building confidence isn't an easy process. You may need more than yourself, your friends, and people on the street to shift your way of thinking. If you really struggle to see yourself in a positive light, seek out a professional doctor or therapist. This is your life, and you are worth it.

This is about you, but it affects everyone around you. Growing your confidence will impact your family and your friendships. Once you're free to be wholly, unapologetically yourself, you'll become more aware of your gifts—all the wonderful qualities within you—and you'll want to share them.

Each of us must take that first step to know ourselves better, appreciate who we are, and be willing to make outward changes to best reflect our inner selves. Whether that step is texting a friend about which leggings to buy or getting a five-minute makeover, it's an important step because all the other steps won't happen without it. Transformation isn't instantaneous—it happens in stages, and it's up to you to push the start button.

Believe in yourself.
You have it within you to make
powerful and unique contributions to the world.
Be confident, be visible, and be seen. Making small
changes is one way to gradually break out of habits,
make intentional choices, and gain the confidence
to be the truest, best version of yourself.

In the next chapter, we'll go beyond outward appearances and take a look inside at our health.

Because when you feel good, you look good, and you do good.

ASK YOURSELF

1) What is the truth about me right now? (If you didn't do that exercise, do it now.)

2) What about myself am I not putting out into the world?

3) What can I do differently to exercise those positive, hidden qualities?

4) If I could change just one thing about myself on the outside to better represent that amazing woman I am on the inside, I would choose to make a change to my (pick one):

   a. Supplement routine

   b. Exercise routine

   c. Makeup

   d. Haircut or style

e.   Clothing

f.   Skincare

5)   Who among my friends can I call for advice?
     Who might be able to help me or might want to take
     this transformational journey with me?

Chapter 3

HEALTHY YOU

After my scoliosis surgery, I lost twenty pounds in just six days. Thinking about that weight loss now, I can't imagine the tremendous toll the procedure must have taken on my sixteen-year-old body. It's scary, and I would never want to lose that much weight that quickly now.

What's even scarier is the response I got, and my reaction. People noticed how thin I was, and instead of being concerned for my health, they complimented me on how good I looked. I don't fault them for this—over the years, I've told plenty of skinny friends how great they look. We're conditioned to believe that "thin is in" and anything else isn't...well, it just isn't good enough.

My teenage body-conscious self was flattered by the attention. What teenage girl doesn't love being complimented on her appearance? Instead of trying to gain back the substantial weight I had lost from a grueling surgical procedure, I convinced myself to do whatever it took to maintain the new body.

For nearly two decades after my surgery, I fell into the diet mentality and rules I had seen in my family for generations. You know the ones: carbs are evil, your dress size must be in the single digits, and you should feel guilty after every meal. It's the toxic mentality that makes Girl Scout cookie season a test of willpower and turns the holidays into a season of extreme anxiety. My goal was to maintain a weight of 128 pounds. Over time, my post-surgery weight naturally increased. It tried to get back to its normal, comfortable, healthy level. But that's not what I wanted.

I worked out excessively and went from one diet to the next, developing disordered eating that impacted my physical and mental health. My self-worth equaled the number 128, and if I didn't see that number on the scale after my morning shower, it was going to be a bad day. Mind you, I only saw that number probably once, and I was holding onto it for decades.

The only times I allowed myself to gain weight were during my pregnancies, but once I was home from the hospital I was right back to dieting, trying to reach that number I would never reach. I wasn't a teenager anymore; I was a young mother who had grown and whose body had changed dramatically. The number I wanted to see on the scale, the number I had allowed to dictate my self-worth, was completely unrealistic. My body wasn't happy or healthy at 128 pounds.

I failed to see what I was doing to myself and stuck to a ridiculous belief about my body and my health. It took years for me to discover that 128 was a big lie, and to find the truth.

You must prioritize your health. Not your weight but your actual *health*. A number on a scale, a dress size, or fitting into the skinny jeans you wore in high school may not be healthy for you. Identify the lies you may be telling yourself, and separate them from the truth. As long as you base your health goals on lies, getting everything else you want for your life will be difficult, if not impossible.

I didn't get healthy overnight. It took time for me to discover the steps that brought me to a healthier, happier, and more beautiful life.

*Real health is how you feel in your body,
not the number on the scale, the size of your pants,
or what you see in the mirror compared to the
edited photos on social media. Your mental
and emotional health are also important.
If you've worked hard and dieted to reach a certain
weight like I did, but you're miserable,
is it really worth it?*

DIET CULTURE

Diet culture that ignores nutrition and instead focuses on achieving the body you were not genetically designed to have, is not a culture of health—despite the message so prevalent in American culture. Women of different shapes and sizes have only recently begun to appear in the media, and even in advertisements for health and beauty products. However, for those of us raised on a diet culture, turning off the belief that "you can't be too thin" is hard to get past.

As I got older and especially after I had children, I thought it was normal to constantly be at war with my body. The daily disappointment—every time I looked in the mirror, stepped on the scale, or shopped for clothes—had my self-esteem at an all-time low. It wasn't until I faced my lies and recognized how unrealistic my weight goals were that I could see the harm I was doing to myself. Not just my body but my emotional self was also suffering. My self-worth suffered. There was actually a point in the last few years, and I'll tell you about it later, that I got really close to that number. But this was before I truly understood what real health was.

For me, the first step toward getting healthy was getting rid of my scale. I made the decision to stop focusing on how far off I was from 128 every day and start focusing on how I actually felt physically, mentally, and emotionally. Then I asked myself, "What is the best health for me? What does it look like?"

I redefined what health looked like *for me* by visualizing my healthiest self. What would a healthy Dana look and feel like? What did I need to do to get from where I was to that person I could become? I had so many questions around diet, exercise, and health routines. I was overwhelmed and didn't know where to start. I needed help.

I had tried fitness challenges in the past, thinking the peer pressure would motivate me to get into shape. I had tried gym memberships too, thinking that working out in a room full of fancy equipment, surrounded by active, fit people would give me a boost. Neither option worked for me—and I never went to the gym. I needed help.

SHOPPING SOCIAL AND A HEALTHIER YOU

Once I made my decision in February of 2021, I turned toward my friends. I wanted to know what the right routine looked like for me. I wanted something that was sustainable, something I could do each day that would get me closer to true health.

I reached out to my friends—my circle, Kelli, Jennie, and Charleigh, who had different pieces of the true health puzzle that I needed. I had watched their journeys to health, and I wanted it too. They were all happy to speak with me about products and services they had discovered through their businesses. While these solutions worked for them, I was afraid they might not work for me. I had so many questions:

1. What if I get my hopes up and this doesn't work?

2. What if I fail? What will that do to my already low self-esteem?

3. What if I invest in a solution and don't get the results I expect? Am I wasting my money?

4. I want to talk to my friends about this, but if I fail, what will they think of me?

5. *Should* I tell anyone? Will my family and friends support me or sabotage me?

I had to overcome my fears, take a risk, and allow myself permission to fail. But I needed to try something. Being brave enough to fail was my only hope for success.

I talked to my circle about food preferences. Their encouragement and advice guided me to dietary choices that worked for me, and they looked nothing like the series of diets I had put myself through (I still eat Chick-fil-A once a week). I also told my circle I preferred to exercise at home by going for walks or doing an exercise video, but every once in a while, I went to a yoga class. We found a routine that worked well for my lifestyle. Best of all, none of their advice involved the daily torture of getting onto the scale or trying to squeeze my grown-up body into teenagers' clothing.

As I enter new stages of life, I continually redefine my approach to health. My routine will never be set in stone because I'm always growing and aging. But I'm not afraid to try new things anymore. I actually enjoy trying new, healthy options, whether it's adding more nutritious foods to my diet or changing up my workout routine. Looking back, I can't believe how much time I wasted fixated on an unrealistic state of perfection, thinking that if I could just reach that goal, I'd be healthy. I could have been doing what I do now: educating myself about what true health means for me and trying different methods to get there. This process was a series of *what ifs*: What if I added this supplement in the morning? What if I added this one in the afternoon? What about this one in the evening? What if I swapped out one of these products throughout the day? What difference might that make?

The most critical change in my approach to health was how I viewed exercise and eating habits. Before, I saw them as chores, and if I didn't do them, I had failed. I would allow myself to feel shame, as if once again, I wasn't succeeding. Self-shaming has to be one of the most nonproductive, and really, self-destructive ways to spend your time. Yet that's how I felt every time I didn't eat the right thing or spend enough time exercising. To *get* healthy, I learned, I had to *think* healthy. That meant acknowledging that I liked feeling good. I liked looking good. I liked being good—the healthier version of myself that I now knew was possible. And absolutely no shame whatsoever, nowhere, and in any way, shape, or form. Once I made that mental shift, I added more women to my circle and continued working on my health. Besides nutrition and exercise, there were hydration and sleep to consider. I found, among my friends, more skilled people to help me find the right products that suited my new way of thinking.

I figured out what questions to ask these experts to reach my goals and was met with equal enthusiasm as they asked *me* questions to finetune their recommendations (and they also always tried to find me the best deals). Without their help, I would probably still be years away from finding the approach to my health that I have now.

Weight Loss

Weight loss shouldn't be the ultimate goal but getting healthy may include losing weight. Be realistic in your weight goals. Your age, frame, and genetics have a lot of say about your healthy weight. Your healthy weight may be 128 (or whatever you weighed in high school) but more than likely, especially if you've had children, you'll feel better with more weight (and muscle) on your bones. Whatever you do, don't set your sights on a cover model or social media influencer and try to match their look. It's their job to look a certain way. It's your job to strive for overall health.

Get clarity on your ideal health, then apply intentionality to reach it. Take control of the foods you eat. Find an exercise routine you enjoy that suits your lifestyle and delivers the results you're after. Rely on your circle to support you.

Getting to a healthy weight isn't a one-and-done process. It's a lifestyle change that gets you to a healthier place and keeps you there with regular maintenance. This may include changes in diet with a focus on balanced nutrition, along with exercise and supplementation. Each person has different needs, so what works for me, or for your best friend, may not work for you. Your circle can help you craft an individual solution tuned to your body.

While a diet focused on a targeted weight goal or dress size may provide immediate, temporary results, health culture is sustainable. This includes immunity and prevention. When you visit your family doctor, how often do they talk to you about what you can do to prevent ill health? More likely, they focus on treating symptoms and providing temporary fixes. Unfortunately, that's a typical experience for many patients. When I realized I was spending more time in the waiting room than with the doctor, I knew I had to take my health matters into my own hands and seek out other sources.

If your doctor prescribes medication without first understanding your overall health, you don't have a doctor—you have a drug dealer. Of course, if you're having a health issue you *should* consult your doctor and follow their advice, but your overall health isn't their first priority. They don't have time in their schedules to discuss diet, exercise, sleep, supplements, and everything else that contributes to your health. You must prioritize all those things and find the time to improve them. Your health is in your hands. You must make decisions and investments today to ensure your health today and in the years to come.

Prepare to Do the Work

I'm not going to sugarcoat it: getting to a place of health is hard. It's extremely difficult on your own, and even with the help of other women to guide you on your health journey, you still must be committed to do the work. First, seek out a team of the right people to help you. Then build your own circle of experts who represent products and services in categories like these:

- Daily nutrition

- Hydration

- Sleep

- Energy

- Daily habits and routines

- Digestion

- Skincare

- Mental health

- Exercise

- Supplements

- Healthy ways to feel your best

- Healthy ways to show up for your kids, spouse, family, and friends

Not only can your circle guide you to great products, but it can also support you through the fear of failure and vulnerability that comes with trying anything new. It was difficult for me, at first, to accept that kind of help. I'm naturally independent, and it isn't in my nature to ask for help or even accept it when it's offered. To get to my healthier self, I had to let down my guard and let other people in, people who had my best interests at heart and truly wanted to make my life better.

HEALTH'S HIDDEN CAUSES RUN DEEP

Poor health may be tied to other problems that have nothing to do with diet and exercise. There may be a physical illness, disease, or other condition impacting your health, and if that's the case, see a professional doctor first.

Poor health may also be caused by external forces. I'm not talking about black mold (though that can certainly cause major health problems) but dysfunction in the household. Growing up, the dysfunction in my family was alcoholism. Living with alcoholism in my home and the unpredictability it brought to my home environment impacted my health. I couldn't control the chaos and confusion around this, so I turned my attention to what I could control, which later in life, was my body. Now I realize that, for me, it wasn't a simple matter of watching what I ate. I was compulsive about it to the point that I probably suffered from eating disorders. I had no one to talk to about it because we never discussed challenges in my family. Vulnerability wasn't common, so we ignored the alcoholism, the depression, and the disordered eating. We pretended everything was fine. I put on a brave face, but inside, I was kind of a mess.

As an adult, I didn't want my own children to grow up with this confusion, so I turned to prayer and therapy. I had to train myself to be vulnerable, to be willing to accept and admit I didn't have everything figured out. My life wasn't perfect, I couldn't control every aspect of it, and that was okay. That transformation was a scary process, but I came out stronger and more confident than I had felt my entire life. Vulnerability, I learned, is not weakness. It's believing you are strong enough to let other people into the darkest places in your life, trusting they won't hurt you, and knowing that even if they do, you are strong enough to survive.

To become healthier, you first have to
work through what's false to find what's true.
Reset your internal health compass and embrace the
freedom to find the products, services, and habits
that deliver a healthier, happier you.

My journey to real health was liberating. I had a new sense of freedom and clarity. For the first time, I could see the lies I had been telling myself for decades. I let go of the shame that accompanied those lies, the fear that came from knowing deep down inside that my fixation with 128 pounds as a goal didn't feel right because it wasn't right. If it wasn't the right goal, then what was? I didn't have it all figured out, and that was okay. I had to get to a place where I believed it was okay to not know, to not have it all figured out, to admit I needed help to find the answer.

I let other people in, and they responded. With care. With guidance. With support. With love. I broke away from the toxicity of a mindset about health that wasn't serving me and created a new mindset that was vulnerable yet confident, open yet strong.

Today, I'm healthier than I've ever been. I sleep better, have more energy, and I feel at home in my body. I had to let down my guard to get where I am, reaching out to friends and allowing them to help me find the routines, haircare, skincare, supplementation, stress management, and spiritual wellness that are all a part of real health.

Whatever toxic beliefs you have about your health, it's time to reject them. Write them down. Scribble them out. You can burn the paper if you like (carefully and in a safe place). Rid yourself of your 128 or whatever it is you've been telling yourself about your health that just isn't true. Only then can you open yourself up to real health and the people who can help you get it.

ASK YOURSELF

1. Who is in charge of your health? You, your doctor, or someone else?

2. What are the lies you've told yourself about your body and health? What are the truths?

3. Envision your ideal health. Do you have the knowledge, the products, and the energy to get there?

4. What about your health would you like to improve first?

5. Who among your friends might help you with that first step? Not only to guide you to products, but to provide motivation and support?

PART TWO

INVITATION

This is your invitation to do something different. I know it can be difficult to break out of our habits and create a new perspective—it's scary to try something new, and even more terrifying to pick ourselves up when our first try doesn't work. But if you've started the process of finding your true health, you will have the resilience needed to invest and extend this to your environment and your family too. Think of it as a ripple effect: becoming the best, truest version of yourself naturally affects those around you, and they benefit from your effort and joy.

This ripple all starts with knowing who you are and what you want and creating this reality. We are the gatekeepers of our homes, and taking a few simple steps can get our families aligned with our visions for true health. This process isn't going to be easy or quick. It will take time to reach your vision for your home, but it's up to you to be flexible until you find what works for your family.

Remember our goal isn't perfection because perfection isn't real. Do we all wish we were sitcom families with the perfectly clean households, perfect meals, and perfect, effortless routines? Of course. Is this attainable? Of course not. You might not have picture-perfect homes, but what you attain will be much better—you'll create the routines, spaces, and healthy mindsets that are perfect for your family and your family alone. If you keep this goal on the horizon, nothing can set you back from reaching what is best for you and your family, not even failures or naysayers who want to discourage your growth.

It's time to get to work.

Chapter 4

HEALTHY FAMILY

On January 9, 2021, my mom had a bad fall. My dad rushed her to the emergency room, and along with the obvious deep cut above Mom's eye, we learned she had broken her spine, a wrist, and a finger. She was beat up big time, and we knew her recovery would be tough. Mom had to wear a Miami J cervical brace for her spine. She had wrist surgery, plastic surgery, many appointments with a hand specialist, and at-home physical therapy.

I wish that were the whole story.

The physical examination included a CT scan that uncovered a mass. Further tests proved the worst: cancer. It had started in Mom's appendix and moved to her ovaries and other organs. When I got the call from my dad, my response was "*F*ck*".

Mom is everything to me—to our whole family. She's my hero and my children's hero. Mom has the heart of a servant, showering us with continuous care, love, and support. The idea that a woman like her could be struck down by something so horrible was unimaginable.

The diagnosis was followed by never-ending medical procedures: a colonoscopy, an appendectomy, abdominal surgery, and chemotherapy. It's been brutal for her and everyone around her. I can't help but think what might have happened if Mom hadn't fallen that day. When would we have discovered the cancer, and would it have been too late?

Soon after my mother's cancer diagnosis, I realized I had to get serious about my family's health—remember Florida, February 2021? In our busy day-to-day lives, trivial matters seem so important: there are emails to answer, groceries to pick up, and social events to attend. That all fades into the distance when you have a health emergency. In the back of my mind, I had thought of my family's health and was doing what I assumed most women did. I made sure my kids didn't eat too much junk food, had vegetables frequently, and spent time playing outside. I had also told myself someday I'd get serious about my family's health.

With the impact my mom's cancer had on my family, I knew that someday was today. The time for me and my family to create a healthier life was now. We didn't have control over everything, but we could make changes to be stronger, healthier, and more immune to disease.

We couldn't prevent every illness or accident, but we could build ourselves up to ward off health threats. If we did get sick or hurt, our healthier bodies would have a better chance of recovery.

As a mother with two young children, most of my days were dedicated to surviving. I didn't have time for made-from-scratch meals or spending a whole afternoon at the park. When my mother had her fall, I had reached that sweet spot in my life when my kids were old enough—six and eight—to not require every minute of my attention. I was out of new-mom survival mode. If you have babies or toddlers, be realistic about what's possible. The demands on your time and energy are high. Sleep may be the only health priority you can reasonably manage. Once the kids are a little older, it's time to make changes. Take the same clarity and intentionality that works for improving your health, and apply it to not only yourself but also your family.

YOU ARE YOUR CHILD'S ROLE MODEL

Kids look to their parents for guidance on how to speak and behave. They pick up on our habits and routines. Our children look up to us and want to be like us. Your teenager might disagree, but science has shown that the most influential people in a child's life are their parents. Because our kids pattern their behavior after ours, it's our responsibility to be good examples for them.

With my schedule, as part of my routine, I drink protein shakes for breakfast every day. They're nutritious, easy, and they save time. My kids have a number of breakfast choices, and they'll often request a protein shake too, instead of waffles, toast, or a bowl of cereal.

They see me drink water all day, and because they're constantly taking sips, I carry a forty-ounce bottle. We joke that Mommy's water is always the best. If I take it, they'll drink it. Similarly, my children see me take supplements and work out, and then they want to do the same. The more mindful you are about your healthy habits, the more likely your children are to adopt the right habits instead of picking up the wrong ones. Have you ever seen a mother smoking cigarettes in front of their young children? Think about the message that sends to the little ones. You are always sending messages to your kids, and always influencing their behaviors now and in the future.

Remember how I told you that alcoholism was a part of my childhood? Well, here's the thing: it was always confusing to me because there was never alcohol in my house. Since I never saw either of my parents drink alcohol, it was not something I ever desired to do. As a result, my husband and I don't have any alcohol in our house either. To be clear, I'm not against drinking. I think it's totally fine if people want to have a drink here and there, but my husband and I just don't drink. We don't like the taste of it because it's an acquired taste we were never introduced to. With both of us growing up with alcoholism in our family, it just doesn't add any value to our family, our lives, or our health.

Choose products that support your healthy choices. This is where my circle can make what seems like a huge task much easier. Your circle can work with you on your family's health goals and recommend the best products for your needs. Even if you just start with yourself, your family will benefit from the changes you introduce. Think about it: I take supplements every morning, and so do my kids. I drink a shake every morning; sometimes they do too. Don't think of the cost as an expense. You are investing in your children so they can be healthier now and develop habits and routines to maintain their health as they grow.

We are the role models and the gatekeepers to our children's health. We decide which products to buy, and we have the power and responsibility to buy the best for the people who mean the most to us. We can settle for drugstore vitamins, shampoo, body wash, sunscreen, and toothpaste, or we can leverage the benefits of shopping social to discover high-quality products for our families.

Just as you envisioned what real health looked like for you, do the same for your family. How do you envision them at their healthiest? Which habits and routines have you modeled for them that they're following? Have they picked up your healthy behaviors? Are there any unhealthy behaviors they're also mimicking?

Your current health professionals—the doctors, dentists, and other medical people—should be supporting you in your quest for a healthy family. If they are not, don't be afraid to find new professionals who go beyond treating illnesses and injuries to treating your whole health.

YOU REALLY ARE WHAT YOU EAT

I can't emphasize enough the importance of nutrition in your family's diet. Food, drinks, and oxygen are your body's main resources. They're what your body uses to create new cells—new skin cells, hair cells, heart cells, and brain cells. That doesn't mean you have to obsess over food though.

My kids still eat fast food and sweets, in moderation. Those foods do not make up a large portion of our day-to-day meal plans. We model good food choices for our kids, but we don't deprive them of all the foods they enjoy either. Diet culture tells us we can never have hamburgers, candy, or dessert. That's unrealistic and could create a feeling of missing out. It teaches children that they have to adhere to a strict diet to achieve health, when that simply is not true. They can find a balance, and developing healthy everyday habits makes that balance easier to achieve.

When the kids come home from trick-or-treating with a pillowcase full of candy, they don't eat it all in one night. When we go to a football game and fill up on hotdogs and nachos, we will likely have a good walk and much healthier meals the next day. Balancing what's fun with what's healthy prevents kids from feeling like healthy eating is a chore. By trying a variety of new foods, they discover many healthy options and often prefer them over less-healthy choices.

Small Changes that Make a Big Difference

You might think personal products such as soap, body wash, and shampoo have little effect on your kids' health, but think about how often they use those products.

How many times a week do you rub that shampoo into your child's scalp? How many times a day do they wash their hands with that liquid soap? Are these products good enough, or is there something better?

- Take an inventory of your bathroom products. Are they brands you're used to and buy out of habit, without putting any real thought into what's best for your family?

- Who among your social seller friends might be able to help you find something better?

Shopping social allows you to work with someone who knows and cares about you, knows how important your family is to you, and will take the time to learn what you need. They will understand if their first recommendation isn't quite right and will work with you to find the optimum solutions for your family's health.

For the next week, track your family's meals and snacks.

- Are they getting enough protein, carbohydrates, and fats? Are they eating mostly whole foods, or is most of the food processed?

- What small exchanges could you make to ensure more nutritious meals and snacks?

You don't have to do away with pizza night or taco Tuesdays. You can choose healthier pizza toppings or better yet, get all the ingredients and make your own, healthier pizza and your own tacos. You can also sign up for a healthy meal subscription service and have all the ingredients and recipes delivered weekly.

CHANGE TAKES TIME

Creating a healthier lifestyle for your family won't happen overnight. It takes time to change behavior, and this is especially true for children who lack the understanding that you, as an adult, have around the importance of health. Take small steps and give everyone time to adjust. Involve them in your decisions. Show your kids the nutritional values of foods and explain how the vitamins, nutrients, proteins, carbs, and fats help them grow into healthier versions of themselves.

Here's the real truth about food: I am not perfect, but I'm not striving for perfection anymore. There were times when I thought about what I could and couldn't have, and I don't live that way anymore. Here's another truth about food: I don't actually cook. I'm good at making a few things and I'll make them every once in a while, but food preparation has mostly fallen to my husband because I don't love it. Even so, we have to decide together what food choices look like for our family. He makes the meals and does the grocery shopping, but we have the same goals for our family. Sometimes that means a homemade meal, but other times it looks like going out to eat.

Making health goals for our family needs to be done together, but it's not always easy. There have been times in the past when I've gone all-in for a new diet, and it was hard for him to come alongside and ask, "How can I support you in this?" when I hadn't considered how he could support it. There were times when I tried programs that took so much preparation and I was in charge of all of the food, for everyone, all the time...even though you already know I don't enjoy cooking. It was overwhelming and it wasn't sustainable. The fact of the matter is you and your partner know what's best for your family and you need to know who is taking on which roles. If you're not the one who's responsible for grocery shopping or for preparing the food, does your partner understand your desires for your health? It might take a while to reach your vision for your family's true health, but the core of success is communication and understanding.

As patient as you must be with the kids, getting your partner on board the health train may pose a bigger challenge. Matt understands when I don't want to get fast food, and he'll pitch in to make healthier homemade meals with me occasionally, knowing it's important to me and better for all of us. He takes on the kids and the household so I can do yoga, follow an exercise video, or go for a walk. We are equally invested in our kids and committed to collaborating for our shared vision of family health.

It might take a while to reach your vision for your family's true health. Not everyone in your house will have the same growth mindset that you do. It's up to you to set the example, be encouraging, and be flexible until you find what works for your partner and your children. Remember the goal isn't perfection. The goal is to take small steps and give others time to adjust. Any progress in your family's health is a win.

IT'S NEVER TOO LATE TO GET HEALTHY

My mom grew up in diet culture. She was constantly on diets as far back as I can remember. She believed she was never thin enough and always felt as though she had more weight to lose. After her cancer diagnosis, she lost at least 30 percent of her body weight. After another accident in November 2021, it was really scary. She was so thin. The number one thing her oncologist said was, "You've got to gain weight. You don't have any strength." For someone who has been on a diet for most of their life, this isn't an easy thing to work through. You would think being told to gain weight would be good news and an easy goal, but my mother still struggles with her diet culture mindset. She's afraid to eat foods that will help her gain weight, thinking they'll make her fat or make her look fat. At sixty-eight years old, she is having to change how she thinks about food so she can learn to eat more of it to stay healthy.

The beliefs around food and weight and health that Mom grew up with still plague her, and I do not want my children to suffer from those beliefs when they are out on their own and no longer under my care. As parents, it is our responsibility to model healthy habits and attitudes to promote their health now and forever.

My mom's cancer diagnosis was the wake-up call I needed to recognize how the health of one family member could impact all of us. Being faced with her mortality reinforced in me that I had to make my family's health a top priority. You don't have to wait for a health scare to put a plan into action. Start today with one small change.

ASK
YOURSELF

1. What healthy legacy do you want to leave for your family?

2. What does health look like for your kids?

3. What do you need to get there?

4. Who are the people who can help you?

5. What divide of health/leisure makes sense for your family? Eighty/twenty? Seventy/thirty? What is your current ratio?

6. What are the practices in your family that you want to moderate, such as screen time?

7. What are some activities you can replace these moderated practices with that will bring your family closer to your vision for true health? For example,

can you cut out some nightly TV time in favor of throwing a ball outside?

8. Are there any communities, in person or online, that you can rely on?

Chapter 5

HEALTHY HOME

My friend Kelli was pregnant with her first child and was cleaning her house one day when she became violently ill. The heavy chemicals in the air created by the cleaning products made her dizzy and sick to her stomach, and she began vomiting. It was terrifying. She didn't know why it was happening, but she had to figure it out. She didn't want this to be something that would impact her unborn child. She started digging into the root cause of why she was getting sick and researching what was in the products she was using to clean her house. Were they helping her, or were they hindering her?

Kelli got rid of the products, but she couldn't help but wonder what the fumes that had made her so ill might be doing to her unborn child. Looking around her home, Kelli thought about the many products she used to clean, disinfect, and deodorize her house. The place looked spotlessly clean, but at what cost? Were the products she used to make her home safer more dangerous than the bacteria and viruses they claimed to neutralize?

The air, floors, carpeting, furniture, surfaces, and all the items in our homes—the toys and electronics—make up an unnatural environment where we live, work, and play. Since COVID, we're spending even more time at home. Instead of leaving the house for work, shopping, and entertainment, we're working remotely, shopping online, and streaming movies. Now more than ever, with many of us spending even more time at home, having a clean house isn't enough. We want our homes to support our health.

HOME HEALTH FOR YOUR HEALTH

We spend a lot of time in our homes. Year after year, we get so used to occupying the same rooms that we practically stop seeing them. We no longer notice the pile of mail on the counter or how awkwardly the living room furniture's arranged. We get used to searching for our purse, our keys, and our phone. We know these things aren't quite right, but we don't give them any thought. We put up with the disorganization and disarray, telling ourselves it isn't a priority. *It just isn't that important. We'll get to it another day.*

Your home environment *is* important. It impacts your health and the health of your family. Think about how you feel walking into a room you've just cleaned up or how you feel opening a cabinet or drawer you've organized. Compare that to the feelings you get walking into a messy room or opening a typical "junk drawer." If it's been a long time since you had a really clean, organized room in your house, think about how it feels to walk into a nice hotel room. The beds are made and everything's neat and tidy. There's no clutter at all—only items that need to be in the room: a bed, a desk, maybe a refrigerator, microwave, coffee maker, and television. The room smells nice too.

Now think about how it feels to come home after staying in a nice hotel. Sure, it's great to be home. You missed your family and maybe the dog. But after being away for a time, the clutter sort of hits you in the face when you walk in the door. You notice the laundry and the paperwork. You notice the shoes on the floor and the dishes in the sink. You might notice the smells too.

You can create a much better home environment, but you might need some help. Family-friendly cleaning products and organizers made specifically to manage the various types of clutter go a long way toward turning the home you exist in to the restful retreat you deserve.

MY HAPPY, HEALTHY HOME

Our house was built in 1956, in the mid-century modern design. The moment I saw it, I knew it was our home. The clean lines and floor-to-ceiling windows felt right, but it wasn't perfect. We needed to gut the entire interior because of the layout. The bedrooms were too big, the bathrooms were tiny, there were too many large closets, and despite all those windows, the layout made the whole place super dark. We ended up gutting the interior to create an open floor plan that matched our vision and made us feel right at home, which is exactly how you should feel when you are at home.

I'm not saying my house is perfect—far from it. The people at *Better Homes & Gardens* haven't come calling, and I don't expect them to. Our home reflects me and my family. It's full of light, life, joy, and fun. You probably don't need to gut your house to create the home you love, like we did. But with intentional decisions, you can create a haven for your family.

Take Inventory

Getting your home into healthy, tip-top shape takes time, but every change you make will feel like a weight off your shoulders. First, get clarity around the kind of home you want to create. Think about how you want your home to make you feel. Then take an inventory:

- Grab that notebook from the earlier exercises, along with a pen. Stand up and look around. How do you feel about this room? Now close your eyes and take a deep breath.

- Jot down your thoughts. Do you like this room? Is it stuffy or airy? Does it make you smile or cringe?

- What about the room would you like to change? Is there something that could be cleaner or more organized? Is there anything in this room you'd just like to get rid of?

- Now close your eyes again and picture the room as you would like it to be. Do you see it? How hard would it be to create the room of your dreams?

- Unless you're fantasizing about a castle in the sky (or a mansion in Beverly Hills), the changes you imagined probably aren't that drastic. Do you see how doable this is?

- Step into the next room, and the next. Write down everything you'd like to change about each one to make it an organized, healthy space that makes you smile.

Use your notes as a first draft of the healthy home you'll create. Don't worry if it's a long list. You don't have to tackle all of it today. Every improvement you make—whether it's cleaning out one drawer, finding a shoe organizer for all of your family's footwear, or getting a paper shredder to take care of all the junk mail—will feel like a weight off your shoulders. Use that feeling to motivate yourself to do more.

TIPS THAT MAKE A DIFFERENCE

Here are some ideas for making your home a happier, healthier place for you and your family. If you need help finding any of these resources, reach out to your circle for advice.

Tip #1: Cleaning Services

Listen, the days of having to do it all on your own are over. No one has the time or energy for feeling exhausted. Can I suggest giving yourself permission for one thing? *Hire someone to clean your house.* Hear me out: I know it's a cost, but please think about it as an investment in a healthier, happier home for your family and more peace of mind for yourself.

We hire someone to clean our house, but we're not extravagant here. It's once a month. And once a month, I know my house is totally clean. Not just the bathroom, not just the living room or one bedroom, but the entire house.

Of course, throughout the month we're keeping up the house, but it's easier when we know it's totally clean once a month. I want to encourage you. I know it can be a stretch. You're worth the investment because what stresses you out more than a messy house is the constant thought in the back of your mind: "I have to clean the house. I have to clean the house. I have to clean the house." It gets old, right? I promise you that hiring someone to clean your house could be the thing that changes your life.

If you do hire a service like we do, talk to them about the products they use. A lot of times you can supply your own. If they bring their own products, talk to them about which ones you prefer in your home and which support your goals for your family. Make sure there is alignment.

Tip #2: Get Organized

An organized home is a stress-free home. That doesn't mean investing in more closet space. In fact, when we redid the floorplan of our house, we removed most of the storage space. That might sound counterintuitive, but I viewed every inch of storage space as an opportunity to collect stuff we seldom used and didn't need. I think about this all the time. In my house, if we haven't used something for a year, it's out of here. We get rid of it.

Think about the places in your home that cause you stress. Do you get anxious every time you dig through your coat closet? Do you hate opening your fridge and searching for what you need? Do you avoid the garage, or stay out of the back yard because there is just so much stuff and you don't know what to do with it?

Reorganizing in steps makes the job manageable. Start by getting rid of items you no longer want or need and then organize what's left. Think about how you'd like to organize the things you keep and look for products that support your vision. Ask friends if they have any recommendations for organizational practices or products and see if they would fit your home as well.

Just like hiring a cleaning service, there is no shame in hiring a lawn care service or a professional organizer. Being a mom, a wife, and maybe having a career doesn't mean we have to do everything else too. Get some help for your home, yourself, and your family.

Tip #3: Your Home as a Sensory Experience

Beyond a clean house, think of your space as a total sensory experience. The décor, furniture, lighting, and even the scent affect how you experience a room. What kind of sensory experience would make you feel most at home?

I like to bring the outside in with windows and natural light. You may prefer a floral theme or a rainforest. Maybe you love your home the most around the holidays when it smells like evergreen and apple pie. Why not enjoy that feeling year-round?

Room fresheners and other natural alternatives like essential oil diffusers can be great additions. They're just one of many options you have for turning your home into a better, healthier reflection of you.

Tip #4: Cleaning Supplies

Typical household cleaners can be unhealthy for you and your family, like they were for Kelli. You can find healthier alternatives through shopping social. Seek out women from among your friends who have similar home health goals and ask them for advice. They may be social sellers, or they may be able to introduce you to women who carry these products.

If cleaning is easy, I'm more likely to do it (between the monthly done-for-me cleaning, of course), so I look for products that make cleaning convenient. For example, my house isn't huge, but it has many windows—eighty-five, to be exact. Can you imagine cleaning eighty-five windows? Through shopping social, I found chemical-free, environmentally friendly quick-wipe cloths that save me a lot of time on those windows. I would never spend hours scrubbing them, but because the wipes make it so easy, the windows stay clean, and we have a lot of sunlight streaming into our home. Clutter, and even smudges on windows, create stress, and I want to feel calm and at peace when I'm at home.

The window cloths don't make me happy. They don't bring me peace and joy. But coming home to a place that's free of stressors helps me relax. That's what I want for my life. Think about what you want. Envision how you want to feel in your home. Then look for people, products, and services to help you create a home that makes you feel that way.

WHAT ARE
YOU WAITING FOR?

You have a right to not feel sick, stressed, worried, or overwhelmed when you walk through your front door. You can create a place of health and rest for you and your family that's in sync with all of you. Don't put this off. You may feel like a healthy home isn't important, but the minute you start the process, you'll understand the difference a healthier home can make in your life. You'll be happier to wake up in it and eager to come home to it.

Think of the nicest hotel you have stayed in. Did *you* deserve that room? Think of the homes of your friends—the nicest homes you love to visit. Do *they* deserve those homes? Of course you did, and they do. You, yes *you*, also deserve a place that makes you happy every day of the year.

Creating a peaceful, restful retreat is
within reach if you give yourself permission to do it.
Look for people, products, and services to help

you take those first steps toward the healthy,
happy home of your dreams.

We've covered a lot of territory so far and I don't want you to feel overwhelmed. Better health for yourself, your family, and your home is a process that takes time. Trust me in this: You are worth it. You deserve a happy healthy life, and with clarity, intention, and a commitment to take care of the most important person in your life—you—you can make it happen.

ASK YOURSELF

1) What is the first step you can take to make your home more comfortable and welcoming?

2) What cleaning products do you use? Are there any you feel you need to swap out?

3) How do you feel about your home's décor? Does it reflect your personality? If not, what are some things you can change to make your home feel more like you?

4) What are some of your favorite scents? What products can you use to make your home smell more inviting?

5) Does your home feel organized? Why or why not? List some specific areas of stress and mess you can tackle, such as organizing your stack of important papers or rearranging a messy fridge.

6) Do you feel like you deserve a restful home? How might your mood and health change if you allowed yourself permission to create the home you deserve?

Chapter 6

WHAT IF I FAIL?

You've invested time, effort, and money into finding recommended products and programs to help you reach your goals. So what do you do if something doesn't work?

The reality is none of us are immune to failure, no matter how intentional we are with our goals. Sometimes things just don't work out. Sometimes you pick the wrong people and products. Sometimes, you pick the wrong goal.

I told you about my so-called "perfect" weight—128 pounds. For years, I convinced myself that if only I could get down to that magical number, my post-spinal-surgery weight, I'd be healthy and happy. My life, at 128 pounds, would be complete.

I left out some of the details.

In 2019, I was in a really tough mental and emotional state. I was still, after so many years, so focused on my weight. I reached out to a friend for help finding yet another diet. She asked me about my goals and then she recommended a diet and exercise plan to help me reach them. Miraculously, after years of trying, I thought I had finally found the perfect solution. I had, in a way, because the plan worked. In a short time, I dropped twenty pounds. For me, weight loss was a way to externally control all of the things I had no control over internally. But then what happened?

Six weeks later, I gained all the weight back.

I felt ashamed, defeated, and guilty. I had invested so much time and effort into losing those twenty pounds, and I had *failed*. I blamed myself, and I blamed the diet and exercise plan. It was a temporary fix, but the weight loss wasn't sustainable. Not for me in my current, post-two-childbirths body. My body was sending me a message: *You're not supposed to weigh 128 pounds. That is not a healthy weight for you.*

The truth is, I felt much better at 148 than I had at 128 (and I still do). I had more energy, and I felt stronger. The only part of me that felt bad was my head, trying to sort out the lie I had hung onto for all those years—that I had to be super-thin to be fit. Regaining that weight didn't make me a failure. That experience helped me gain clarity around true health and led me to make more intentional choices about the decisions I made to be healthy. After that, none of those decisions involved fixating on the scale. I was done.

Not everything you try will work out.
You will experience what seem to be failures on your
journey to true health. These are not failures—they are
steps that bring you closer to what you really need.

Not every product will do what you expect it to do. Your friend's favorite new skincare routine, for example, has transformed her troubled skin, and you can't seem to get that same glowing complexion on your own face. You try the same routine with the same products, and your skin breaks out! Your friend isn't lying, and she didn't recommend a bad product. It just isn't the right product for your skin. When that happens, you're going to feel disappointed, frustrated, and discouraged. Don't give up so quickly. Talk to her about the outcome and let her find something better suited for your skin, or try a different solution from another friend—we have options here, ladies!

Sometimes the product is perfect but the approach is wrong. You purchased an exercise plan, and every morning you're working out as hard as you can. After a few weeks of 5:00 a.m. workouts, you're losing motivation. You aren't used to getting up that early, and you just want to sleep in. You can move your routine to 5:00 p.m. and see whether you're better able to stick with it.

When something fails, you know what *not* to try next and are that much closer to finding the right solution.

THOUGHTS ON "FAILURE"

I know I'm not the only one who has done this. I go to the mall, grab five or six things off the racks, and try them on in the dressing room. Standing in that cramped, carpeted room, I look at everything I'm getting and think the trip was a total success. (If you're like me, you usually find one thing and buy it in three or four different colors, but that's beside the point.) I go home, try everything on again, and end up returning nearly half of what I bought.

I have a theory this is because when we're shopping from endless options, we're pressured in that moment to choose something so we take our best guess. Every time we make a decision, we're assuming we're making the *right* decision. A lot of the time, it turns out we didn't make the right decision because, once we're in the isolation of our home and away from the overwhelming options, we realize what we bought doesn't work.

It's different when I'm buying clothes from one of my friends, which I do often. I've found a brand I really love, and I feel phenomenal in it. I've invested hundreds of dollars in clothing from this brand. Even though I know the brand and how it fits on my body, there are still times when something isn't quite right. What I do return is a handful compared to the mountain I normally return to the mall.

We have to be okay with even these small failures. Many times, when we buy from our friends or make an investment in ourselves that maybe we haven't made before, we expect it to be perfect right away—and it never lives up to our expectations. Remember, perfection doesn't happen right out of the gate.

CURIOSITY

Curiosity is not failure. Curiosity is necessary. We need to be curious about why something is working or isn't working to understand our bodies, to understand our needs, to understand our rhythms, our routines, our habits, what needs to stay, and what needs to go. Every failure showed me I was lying to myself about my needs and abilities and brought me closer to the truth.

To find true health, shift your perspective of failure from "incompletion" to "growth opportunity." Failing isn't really failing if you've learned something and have discovered a truth about yourself.

If you define failure as incompletion and success as reaching your true health, then dropping a program that holds you back from what actually fits your needs is a success. What's the point of finishing a program that makes you miserable and doesn't bring you closer to your goals? Take a deep breath, let the guilt go, and put your energy into finding the right solution.

We live in the woods on twelve acres. It is such a gift. It really is, but it's also a lot of work. Matt is constantly out cleaning the trails and chopping up trees because there are always some that have fallen down. You've heard the cliché, "can't see the forest for the trees." We live in this. Every failure is like a fallen tree, and that's what we tend to focus on. Pretend you're flying a drone over our twelve acres, a forest of possibilities. The fallen trees cut a swath through that forest—a path to achievement. When you're down on the ground in the middle of the forest, you see only the fallen trees. You have to zoom out to see how far you've come.

No doubt you've experienced failures outside of nutrition and exercise programs and the right clothes. I know I sure have. But the concepts around failure still apply. I remember scouring the beauty aisles at big-box stores, looking for deals on the perfect makeup for my complexion.

For a moment, picture yourself at Target. You're walking through the aisles: the shampoo aisle, the soap aisle, the toothpaste aisle, the supplement aisle, the skin care aisle, the makeup aisle. How do you know which products to buy? How do you know which shampoo is going to do what you actually want it to do? How do you know which concealer is going to cover just the way you want it to cover? How do you know which mascara is going to make your lashes look just the way you want? How do you know which supplements will fill the nutritional gaps you know you have?

How do you figure that out? I couldn't. I spent endless hours in these aisles before I made the decision to work with social sellers and create my circle. I ended up with drawers full of failures. Sometimes I kept using them anyway because I felt guilty wasting money. Even if I did, the odds of finding something better on my own were slim.

This is where shopping social really shines. If a product doesn't work for you, talk to your seller. Tell them what you liked about the product and what didn't work for you. Give them a chance to find a more fitting solution. Ask them to refer you to another social seller with a solution more in tune with your personal needs. You don't have to be the expert, especially when you have access to people who are.

Shopping social is intentional shopping. It's knowing you're working with someone who listens to your problems and your goals and helps you find the right solution. It's shopping with confidence, knowing if a product isn't quite right, it's a risk-free step toward a better product for you. My circle sees me as a person with a problem to solve, a goal to achieve instead of a transaction to complete.

Plan for Failure to Achieve Success

When something doesn't work out, we can be too discouraged to keep trying. Think of social shopping as a process. It's not like putting a coin in a slot and having your perfect life pop out. You have to commit to success by planning for the failures and working with your circle to get what you want.

If a product doesn't work for you, don't wallow in failure. Your circle's goal isn't to sell more product—it's to find the right solution for you, make you happy, and keep you coming back for more.

Take an active role in getting what you want. Remember you are worth it. If a product doesn't solve your problem or get you closer to your goal, reach out to your seller. They love hearing success stories, but they need to hear about what doesn't work too. Your feedback helps them become better at what they do so they can guide you and others to better solutions.

- If a product doesn't deliver the results you expected, reach out to the social seller. Make sure you are using it properly and have waited long enough to see results.

- If you're using the product correctly and should have seen results, make a list of what you like and don't like about the product so you can give your social seller clear feedback. For example, you might love a face cream's scent and feel, but it makes your skin break out. Or you may have found a cream that does wonders for your skin, but you hate the scent.

- Talk to your seller and be specific about what you like and do not like in a product. Work with them to identify ingredients that don't agree with you and find products with ingredients that deliver the results you're looking for.

- Don't feel guilty about returning a product or making a seller work for your business. A good social seller is invested in your health goals, not their sales goals.

- Consider keeping a diary of the different products you try and the outcomes. Celebrate the victories. Celebrate the failures too, and the lessons learned you could leverage to find better solutions.

DEALING WITH NAYSAYERS

Failure is best friends with naysayers. People who love you, who hate you, and who are indifferent to you will try to sabotage your plans. Change makes people uncomfortable. They see you taking risks and being vulnerable, and that makes them uncomfortable. Or they see you investing in yourself to make a better life, and that makes them uncomfortable too. They feel intimidated: Will they lose their friend when she fails? Will they lose her when she succeeds and doesn't want to hang out with them anymore? You're doing something different, and they don't know what to expect. It's not you they're sabotaging— it's what might happen to them whether you fail or succeed.

Maybe your spouse isn't fully on board when you could really use their support. Maybe friends or coworkers offer their unsolicited opinions and backhanded remarks about your weight loss, hairstyle, or wardrobe. People who don't have your best interests at heart, and people who do, but whose self-esteem is so low they can't bear to be around others who are doing well, might actually want you to fail.

That's them. This is you. This is *all about you*. The choice to grow and make changes to yourself and your life that bring you health, happiness, and fulfillment is yours. No one else gets a vote. They don't live in your body and experience your life. You have every right to have the best life experience possible, and no one can take that away from you—unless you let them. They're entitled to their opinions, but you're entitled to your growth.

*Failure is an opportunity for us to listen
to ourselves and understand what we truly need.
What's most important is that you keep trying to reach
your vision for true health for yourself and your family
because the results far outweigh the effort.*

PATIENCE IS MORE THAN A VIRTUE

When it comes to positive change, patience isn't just a virtue—it's mandatory. I tried several nutritional plans and exercise routines before landing on what worked for me, and as my life changes, my plans change. My children are less dependent on me now, so I have more time. Some days, work takes a toll and I need more energy or more sleep. Each time I make a change, I have to be patient and give the new plan or routine time to work.

Perhaps even more importantly, making the shift from "every product must be a slam dunk" to "every product is a step in the process to find a healthier me, a healthier family, a healthier home" demands patience. Don't expect to accept this belief overnight. We've all become way too accustomed to instant gratification and results. The human body doesn't work that way. It's on its own time clock and doesn't care about your deadlines. Give your body time to adjust, and it will pay you back with high dividends.

Creating the life you want can require a lot of effort and energy. Doing it on your own can be challenging, exhausting, draining. And yet the hope for a brighter, more fulfilling future pushes us through the struggle. I can't promise this process will be easy. What I *can* promise you is that if you don't back down, if you fight through your failures, if you accept that you and your family are worthy of investment, you will achieve the results you're looking for.

ASK YOURSELF

1) Make a quick list of goals or products that have failed in the past year. For example, did you get a gym membership but barely use it? Why do you consider it a failure? Now, focus on the positives: What did you learn? How did what you thought you wanted reveal what you actually need?

2) What's your definition of failure? What's your definition of success? Do they line up with your goal for true health?

3) What things have you tried that have failed? Why were the results not what you were looking for? Did you think you were wanting one thing, but in the process realized you wanted something different?

PART THREE

CHANGE

We all know change doesn't happen overnight. You can't plant a single seed and wake up the next morning with a lush, overflowing garden—it takes day after day of planting, watering, weeding, fertilizing, and effort for the flowers to bloom. It's the same when we're planting the seeds in our daily lives through the routines we create and the products we invest in.

The good news is there are people who are willing to work with us to figure out exactly what changes will help us reach our personal goals. When we're intentional about what changes we want to make and whom we support, we can make the right investments that create long-term results. When we support our friends, we experience growth beyond what we could have imagined. Stop relying on messaging to tell you what changes you *should* want. Trust yourself to know what you want—then look to real people in your life, in your circle, to help you find the products and services that will help you reach your goals.

You don't have to be stuck. If you unapologetically chase what you know is best for you and your family, I promise that all of the work along the way will pay off in a big way. All it takes is the first little sprout to poke out of the dirt—the first real result from your hard work and carefully curated routines—to give you the encouragement to keep going.

It's impossible to overstate the influence of community. I've seen what shopping social has done for me, and I couldn't have gotten to where I am today without this incredible network of support.

Growth takes strength, courage, and a little help from our friends.

Chapter 7

REAL
RESULTS

Before I took charge of my life, something was always off. Until I got clarity, I couldn't visualize the life I wanted. I could only see many individual challenges standing in the way of health for myself, my family, and our home. I felt like a victim of my circumstances. I wanted to change, but figuring out what I wanted and how to get it were overwhelming. Finding solutions, forming new habits, and adding new routines without any guidance takes time and effort—and mine were in limited supply.

I felt like I was treading water, being hit with wave after wave. I'd start to think about one problem, and before I could get to a solution, another wave would come along and try to drown me. I had to make myself stop fighting the waves and just float for a while: float and think. Figure it out. Write down what I wanted my life to look like and then take on each wave, one at a time. By focusing on just one wave as it rolled in and floating over it instead of fighting it, I reached calmer waters.

Finding the right products, programs, and routines takes time and intentionality. I'm grateful I have found the right solutions to help me feel great most of the time. There are occasional days when I don't get enough nutrition or sleep, and of course, that messes with my health. But those days are few and far between.

My routine consists of lots of water and lots of sleep. (Bless those of you who don't require a lot of sleep. I need nine hours, minimum.) I also have the right exercise routine that fits what my body needs each day. Some days I go for a walk, and other days I go to a yoga class or do a thirty-minute at-home workout. It's never boring and the variety and flexibility suit my lifestyle. Instead of reacting to problems, I invested in preventative health habits. The results are clear: I've been sick much less often, and so have my kids.

When I started this process,
I knew things could get better, but I never imagined
I could be as happy, confident, and strong as I am today.
I put in the work and made dramatic changes to my life.
With clarity, intentionality, and commitment,
you can too.

I feel healthier than I ever have, and those results come from choosing the right products, programs, and routines, and consistently sticking to them. I made a long-term investment in myself for long-term results. Getting to that place in my head and with my emotions—the desire and fortitude to do the work and be at peace with it—took a lot of preliminary work. I had to understand my whole health—physical, intellectual, emotional, and spiritual. You can get there many ways. One particular method worked well for me.

ENERGY MANAGEMENT AND REPLENISHMENT

When working with my LifePlan clients, an area we really focus on is full engagement. The ability to fully engage with others comes not from better time management, like many people assume, but from energy management and replenishment. To better understand what I mean by full engagement, consider that I grew up with two parents who worked full-time during my entire childhood. The thing is, I never felt alone because when my parents were home, they were fully engaged in what was going on. They spent time with my sister and me, and we enjoyed each other's company. It wasn't endless, the time we had together, but it was the right amount of time because my parents had the right kind of energy. This is what an active replenishment cycle allows us.

In the book *The Power of Full Engagement*,[3] author and psychologist Dr. Jim Loehr, who specializes in performance psychology, introduces a concept he developed called PIES. It focuses on a person's physical being (P), intellectual being (I), emotional being (E), and spiritual being (S). Loehr believes that by balancing these four aspects, we can be fully present in our lives. Again, this isn't about managing time, but managing energy.

So what does investing in your energy look like?

First, P: This looks like making sure each one of your days, or maybe each week, has some sort of physical aspect. This could be exercise, good sleep habits, proper hydration, or mindful eating and nutrition.

Second, I: For your intellectual investment, this is anything that grows your mind. Are you listening to podcasts or sermons? Are you reading books or learning a new language or skill? Are you having in-depth conversations with other people?

Third, E: When considering your emotional health, do you see a therapist? Are you regularly getting together with friends? Are you connecting with your spouse so they can support you emotionally? Emotional health might also include creative activities like drawing, painting, or making music.

---

[3] Jim Loehr and Tony Schwartz, *The Power of Full Engagement: Managing Energy, Not Time, is the Key to High Performance and Personal Renewal* (New York: Free Press, 2003).

Fourth, S: When investing in your spiritual self, ask yourself what your spiritual life looks like and how you're growing spiritually. This could be spending quiet time meditating or journaling. It might include some sort of volunteer work. You can also invest in your spiritual health by reading scripture or praying.

It's easy to neglect any one of these areas, so you have to consciously make the effort to intentionally ensure that your physical, intellectual, emotional, and spiritual health don't suffer. Neglecting just one of these areas can leave you feeling exhausted and not like your best self, but once you get into the habit of regular energy management and replenishment, you'll feel more fully engaged in life and with the people around you.

This looks different for everyone, and without actively managing our energy, we all tend to be a little off-balance. Some people might totally invest in their physical health and have a great exercise plan, nutrition plan, and sleep schedule—but are totally depleted from an emotional standpoint. They know that to be their best self, they have to find the emotional support they need.

My Replenishment

I'm an introvert. For me, energy replenishment meant having at least one night at home by myself every month, which every parent knows is hard. When I first laid out my plan for investing in my replenishment, I had a one-year-old and a three-year-old. I was working full time, so my husband Matt was already spending more time with our kids than I was. I had to figure out how to tell him, "I know I might not have the quantity of time as a family that you do, but I know I need this personal time in order to fill myself up so I can fully engage with you and the kids when we are together." Now Matt recognizes when I need a night by myself. He knows I need to recharge in order to be my best self. Not because I don't want to be with my family, but because time alone fills me up.

One weekend, my husband and kids visited a friend for two nights, and I was able to access everything that filled me up: I went for a walk, got my nails done with my mom, and went to a movie by myself. I had the luxury of being able to take naps and read books. By the end of those two days, of course, I missed my family and wished I could have spent the weekend with them. But I was so, so full. I felt like I could give my all for the next three or four months.

Your Replenishment

You might be on the complete opposite end of the spectrum, and instead of needing time alone, you need to be with friends three or four times a week to be filled up. Recognize those things that replenish your energy and fill you up instead of allowing yourself to be drained.

An efficient way to invest in yourself is by adding a habit or routine that nourishes more than one aspect of your being. For example, ask a friend to join you in a weekly yoga class, then go out for coffee and a conversation after the class. Join a book club or Bible study group and start each meeting with five minutes of stretching. You can double up on investments by yourself too, by going for a walk and making a mental list of everything you have to be grateful for in your life. Add long-term habits in each of the aspects of your being for long-term results.

I want to challenge you to identify which of these areas—physical, intellectual, emotional, and spiritual—you feel are not full. It takes all of these things coming together to have your best energy, to be your best self, and to show up the best you can for yourself and those you love. If you can't show up for yourself, you can't show up very well for anyone else.

Find What Works for You

You can get awesome results from programs that don't just nurture you physically, intellectually, emotionally, and spiritually, but offer community. Your initial focus might be on your physical body, but the community support you receive will help you grow in other aspects of your life. When you join a group of caring people with similar goals and who support each other, expect the results to be bigger than you imagined. If you don't want to join a whole group, find one friend—an accountability partner—to come along on your journey.

Reach out to people you know who have experienced personal transformations. Ask for their guidance and encouragement. There was likely something that flipped their switch and turned them away from settling for their situation to going after what they deserved.

Real results don't come in a bottle, or even in a book. If you read this chapter and do nothing, your life will not change. Results are the product of time and effort committed to finding and following what works for your life and delivers what you really want and need. You cannot just will yourself to follow a plan either—you need the right mindset to flip that switch from "wanting results" to "making results happen." If you need help flipping the switch, try this replenishment method, or find another method to connect your wants to haves and turn your wishes into action.

VULNERABILITY AND GROWTH

I struggled for a really long time with any sort of vulnerability. I didn't want anyone to know I was struggling. I didn't want to admit I was setting unrealistic expectations for myself. I didn't want to admit being a full-time working mom with an infant and a toddler was hard.

I didn't admit any of these realities that resonate with a lot of women.

Now, I realize the greatest growth comes from admitting that I don't have it all figured out. I have to allow other people to come alongside me with the encouragement I can't always find within myself. When you're vulnerable with people who care about you, they come through for you. Sometimes they offer support and solutions you didn't know you needed. By being vulnerable, I found community with other growth-minded people. I also found products that work, routines that work, and a new life that fits me—not a life that I was trying to fit into. If you feel like you're on the outside looking in, you don't have to stay there.

Look to women who are vulnerable, women who are transforming their lives for the better and are open to talking about it. These women don't put themselves out there to brag—they're happy. They're changing their lives and can't keep it to themselves. Instead of feeling intimidated by them, why not join them? Put yourself out there and ask them what they're doing. Did they try a new product, a nutrition program, or some new exercise routine? Are they taking a class or learning a new skill? What are they excited about that you might be excited about too, if you could make it happen for yourself?

As I've undergone my own change, I've learned the true beauty of vulnerability and growth. I highlight the positive aspects of my life in conversations with friends and on social media, but I also tell the real story, and it's not all rainbows and sunshine every day. I'm no longer afraid of showing my real self instead of hiding behind a picture-perfect life that doesn't exist.

When I first started sharing honestly and openly on social media, people asked if I was okay. We're so used to seeing everyone's best side—even when that side is a fraction of reality—that we're concerned when we get a glimpse into the other side. I had the same insecurities, the same shortcomings, and the same questions as many women. When I allowed my truth to break through the veil of social media, some people were startled. Did they really believe my life was perfect? I hope not. But now, with the truth out there, they knew it wasn't. I felt better—more honest—putting it out there, and once they realized I was okay, my friends felt better about me and about themselves. Not one of us has it all together. Remember that when someone pretends they do. There is always something else going on, and we must be kind to each other and provide our friends with a safe place to be vulnerable so that in time, they can share their truths too.

The Truth About Me, Part 2

Revisit the list you made in chapter 2's exercise, "The Truth about Me Right Now." Update your list with what you know to be true about yourself right now. Share the list with a friend, your family, or your therapist, and ask them to add to it. Ask them to create their own and add to their lists. Be vulnerable and see how they respond. When you lead with vulnerability by example, others will feel safe enough to be vulnerable too.

FIND WHAT
WORKS FOR YOU

It wasn't until I went through the hard process of recognizing what did and didn't work that I found my results. Identify what you want, what you need, and what you're looking for. They're not always the same thing. As you get to know the real you, these things will change.

Think about all that we've covered so far: clarity, knowing yourself and being seen, intentionality, finding true health for yourself, your family, and your home. To see results in these categories, you need clarity about what makes the most sense for you and your family.

I wanted preventative health for my family, so I intentionally invested in supplements, food, and exercise habits to support my vision of true health. I swapped out old products for new ones that supported our health, and now my family doesn't get sick as often.

Finding real results requires a lot of small steps, such as making the decision to add an immunity-support vitamin into my routine, but it builds up to huge changes. It's not going to happen overnight: taking one vitamin isn't going to make much of a difference at all. It's the commitment to trying, day after day, to make changes that earn the results.

REAL PEOPLE HELP US FIND
REAL RESULTS

Even when you know exactly the results you want, it's difficult to know which products are right for you. We have so many decisions to make in so many areas—clothing, makeup, skincare, diet, exercise, sleep, supplementation—and it's impossible to be experts in all of them. We're forced to trust the marketing smokescreen, which makes it difficult to find the right products.

I prefer to put my faith in real people who have used the products, not the marketing on the front of the package. If you walk down a shampoo aisle, every bottle promises to make your hair strong and shiny. But we know that none of them work the same. It's the personal testimonials that cut to the truth behind the claims on the bottle.

Real people help us find real results. Instead of making a lot of wrong guesses about the products you want to bring into your life, turn to the people who are willing to work with you to find the right things. If you don't get it right the first time, you have the security of knowing you'll get a refund and personalized problem-solving until you get the results you want.

Everyone who has found their real results did so because they gave themselves permission to do things differently, to be vulnerable and try something new. They connected with real people who cared about their goals. Give yourself permission.

You won't experience the results you want
until you take the first steps. Trying something new
is scary, but it's better than staying stuck.
Change your habits and find what works for you.
Only you have control over your life.

I was able to create the perfect routine for myself because I was willing to be vulnerable, identify my needs, and find what habits met them. Mentally go through your day. What habits do you have? What do you wish you had time for, and what do you want to do less? Results all start from changing your routine and finding what supports you physically, intellectually, emotionally, and spiritually.

1. Make the decision to do today what you wish you had done yesterday.

2. Commit to do the same tomorrow.

3. Repeat steps one and two until these actions become habits—part of your routine. Make these actions part of who you are. Be that person.

If you put in the work, one day you'll realize that who you want to be is who you have become.

ASK YOURSELF

1) What comes to mind when you think of the real results you want to experience?

2) What is something you want, and what is your plan to reach that result?

3) What's one small thing you can change in your routine?

4) How do you decide which products to buy? Is your decision based on price or advertising? What if you had a personal testimony or recommendation? Would that make you more confident about your purchase?

5) Are there people in your life who have changed their lives? You may have dismissed these people, maybe even rolled your eyes at them. You may have even tried to sabotage their success.

What if you connected with them instead, and supported them? What if you asked them to help you reach your goals?

6) Think about your replenishment: the physical, intellectual, emotional, and spiritual aspects of your life, of yourself. How can you nourish each one?

7) Who in your life do you admire for their personal transformation? If you were to choose someone to be an accountability partner, who would it be? What's holding you back from sending them a text right now?

8) Visualize a day when you have the energy to be fully engaged. What would you accomplish? How would you feel? What is it going to take to get there?

9) Look at your "The Truth about Me Right Now" list. How can your daily choices support these truths? For example, if you wrote down "I'm naturally curious," is there a class you could sign up to learn something new, and support your intellectual growth?

Chapter 8

SUPPORTING FRIENDS THROUGH SHOPPING SOCIAL

When I was a kid, shopping social was a regular part of our lives. We supported our friends who sold products, and it not only felt good to get high-quality products we needed, but we also enjoyed supporting our trusted friends who represented these products.

My mom would ask me to swing by Fred's house, where he kept a bin on his porch filled with his customers' orders. Fred didn't do home delivery, but he lived down the street and I loved picking through that bin to find Mom's latest purchases. His soap, skincare, body lotion, and makeup brands were always just what we wanted.

For my sophomore homecoming, my date's mom, a social seller, did my makeup using her beauty products. I felt so glamorous, like I had a professional makeup artist who had taken the time to figure out exactly what worked for me. This was much better than going to a random makeup counter, crossing my fingers, and hoping for the best.

For one reason or another, as I entered adulthood I fell out of shopping social. I lost touch with the social sellers Mom ordered our products from and became a big-box consumer. I didn't realize how much more difficult it would be to decipher the truth from the overblown marketing claims about products. I also began to realize that companies can say just about anything about their products, and they expect consumers to believe it. The sad thing is we often do. Again, I'm reminded of bottles of shampoo that promised thicker, shinier hair, and the labels that claimed I was about to buy the world's best-fitting jeans. Nine times out of ten I was disappointed. Shopping like this was like wearing a blindfold and throwing a dart, hoping it would hit the bullseye. It was exhausting, and I was frustrated. Still, I continued making weekly trips to those stores, wasting my time and money on products that seldom lived up to their promises, or my expectations.

Before becoming a corporate consultant for social selling businesses, I lived in Austin, along with my husband, where I worked for an organization that held events for entrepreneurs. I loved working with these new business owners. It was exciting to see so many people starting their own companies and navigating the many roles required to run a business: CEO, marketing specialist, bookkeeper, and so on. I also felt something for these people because what they were doing was incredibly difficult: building a company from scratch with no products or business structure. They had no training or mentors, and most of them didn't have business degrees either. They were winging it for the most part—figuring it out as they went along. Some succeeded, and many failed.

When we moved from Texas to Michigan, I wanted to continue working with entrepreneurs. But I did not want to see so many of them struggling with no one to turn to for help. That's when I remembered Frank's bin. I remembered the lady who sat by the pool, showing my mom and her friends which colors of makeup were most complementary to their complexions. Back then, they called what Frank and that woman did "direct selling." It's still called that, though I prefer social selling because what they did and what direct sellers still do is much more social than direct. They engage with people. Social selling was a way for entrepreneurs to run their own businesses without all the startup hassles. With social selling, you had a product and a company behind you that supported the product and you. I wanted to support these people, so once again, just like Mom, I became a social shopper.

RECLAIMING MY SHOP SOCIAL ROOTS

I never imagined that returning to my roots would change my life. Before quitting the big-box stores, the departments stores, and occasionally, the drugstores, I spent a ridiculous amount of time reading labels, sifting through marketing messages and ingredients to find what I thought was the right product. Still, I was never sure if the product would meet my expectations. Surely, there were skincare, haircare, makeup, nutrition, and exercise solutions that met all my needs and lived up to my expectations. How much money and time would I have to spend to find them?

Another reason I turned to shopping social was the relationships my mother had with her sellers. They cared about her. She wasn't just a consumer or a customer—she was their friend. They took good care of her, and she supported them. As I began reaching out to social sellers among my friends and acquaintances, I got that same feeling. I found women who cared about me and wanted to help me find the perfect products, programs, and routines for my needs and my lifestyle. I developed strong relationships with these women. They're my friends, and they're also my personal shoppers, always looking out for the best solutions for what I need. There is no pressure for me to buy anything, and whenever I'm not 100 percent satisfied, I return the product and they help me find a better one.

Instead of gambling with products, my informed circle of social sellers find products that work. I don't have to wander up and down aisles, reading labels. Just a quick call, text, or email, and my social seller is ready to fill another order for me or discuss something new. It's fast, easy, and actually fun knowing I'm supporting an entrepreneur who has my best interests at heart.

Eventually, I cleaned up my product graveyard. I went through all the drawers, cabinets, and cupboards, tossing beauty products, health-care products, cleaning products, and other personal and household supplies in a tall kitchen garbage bag. I had to get a second bag. These were all products I had stopped using months prior because they just didn't work for me. I don't know why I hung onto them for so long. Maybe I felt guilty, like I was being wasteful. But this time, throwing away all that stuff, I didn't feel guilty at all. I felt lighter. Like I was getting rid of years' worth of dashed expectations and broken promises. I wasn't just cleaning my house—I was clearing out the cobwebs in my head that had been clouding my vision and preventing me from reaching my goals. I was making a statement: No more settling. No more wasting money on what doesn't work. From now on, I am investing in what does work for me and for my family.

Once you build your circle of social sellers, you'll be surprised at how quickly you can clean out all your cabinets too. You'll be investing in solutions that make your life better, enjoying real relationships with people who care about you, and supporting entrepreneurs who have great products and provide awesome service.

Shopping social isn't like trusting a snake oil salesperson.
It offers effective solutions for your life and supports
people who stand behind their products and
care deeply about your wellbeing.

Social selling is more than a job: these sellers truly believe in their products. Many of my friends who are social sellers are at the highest ranks within their companies. They entered direct selling because a product changed their lives, and they're passionate about sharing that change with others.

Invest in yourself, invest in the right products, and invest in your friends and their families. When I look at everything these friends have accomplished, I am so proud of them and grateful for the chance to benefit from them.

FROM DIRECT SELLING TO SHOPPING SOCIAL

At some point, the direct selling channel developed a bad reputation. We've all heard the horror stories of sellers who focused solely on the business opportunity and recruiting other sellers. The skepticism around social selling is deserved, or it was in the past. My dad still has a negative perception of it after a seller aggressively pitched a business opportunity to him even though he made it clear he wasn't interested and already had a job he loved. Because of that experience, Dad wrote off the entire industry. My husband, Matt, supports my work as a consultant in the industry, but he also came to shopping social with a lot of skepticism. His own father had a bad experience many years ago.

You've probably had your own uncomfortable experiences with direct selling. Maybe a friend invited you over for dinner and before you had even finished your salad, they launched into a pitch. Or they invited you to a party to check out some products and then tried to recruit you to sell for them. Or those old acquaintances from high school began awkwardly sliding into your DMs. It's not okay to mislead your friends or pressure them into buying from you or selling for you.

Listen, I've seen it all. I've watched the documentaries and the YouTube videos. I've read the articles about everything that is *wrong* with this channel. Some of it is warranted and weird. And some of these antics still go on. Frankly, people who do this are an embarrassment to the industry. They do much harm to the trust people like me and the social sellers I work with have spent years building between companies, sellers, and shoppers.

This is not what shopping social is about. The people I'm talking about, my circle, and the people I hope you'll find too, are social sellers who genuinely care about us. They want to help you solve your problems, reach your goals, and change your life. Good sellers ask the right questions and listen to your answers. They don't spout buzzwords and try to trick you into buying something you don't need.

You might have reasonable skepticism about direct selling, but don't let your bias close you off from fantastic sellers who care about you, value your friendship, and want to help.

BECOMING A SOCIAL SHOPPER

I am not a social seller, and I have no desire to become one. I am, and will always be, a social shopper. I consider shopping social, first and foremost, as a solution to help me become my best self. I chose to work on the corporate side of the industry to help sellers better educate their shoppers because I understand how hard entrepreneurship can be, and I believe in what these women (and men) do.

Many of my friends have found financial freedom through social selling, and I'm proud to support them. I won't try to convince you to become a seller, but I hope you leave this book a smarter shopper.

Over the years, I not only became a smarter shopper—I also developed a network of friends with whom I have deep, trusting relationships. Shopping social has given me a way to support my friends, and it has been so rewarding to be a part of their growth. Forming real connections and getting great products that have changed my life have inspired me to champion these social sellers—my friends—whenever I have the chance. I am committed to changing my own life for the better while supporting their businesses, livelihoods, families, and communities.

I've seen women change their lives through shopping social, and on the other side, through selling. My friends have paid off their vehicles, their homes, and their student loans, and have enjoyed family vacations with the money they earned through their businesses. I get a huge kick out of supporting that. Their success is my success and vice versa. That might sound too idealistic, but think about it. How does it feel when you help someone else attain their goals? When you become your best self and they helped you get there? When you truly care about your impact, it's the best feeling in the world. Social sellers really do care about your outcome because they know the power of their products.

To become your best self, all you have to do is let them be a part of the process. Trust me, your real friends love nothing more than to help you thrive. Without social selling, I wouldn't be where I am today, and I am so grateful for the help on my journey.

Real friends want to help you.
At its core, shopping social isn't about the money
your friends are trying to make—
it's about helping you become your best self.
When you're intentional about what you need and
who you support, you'll grow in ways
you never thought possible.

I wasted years of my life on products, programs, and routines that fell far short of my expectations, and it bothers me to see so many people doing the same: crowding stores or buying products online from people and companies they don't know. Making the switch from consumer to investor, from uninformed shopper to social shopper, was one of the best decisions I ever made. I had to get clarity and I had to be intentional. I had to care enough about myself, my family, and my household to take that first step, but once I did, there was no going back. Every time one of my social seller friends pays off a debt or a car payment, or can now afford private school for their children, I get an extra lift, knowing I played a small part in their success. I made a difference in my friends' lives, and you can make a difference in the lives of your friends when you embrace shopping social.

ASK
YOURSELF

1) List your goals for your:

    a. Confidence

    b. Health

    c. Family

    d. Home

2) Make a list of the people in your circle who represent products. Which of them might have something that will help you reach your goals in each of these categories? Commit to initiating a conversation with each of them about your:

    a. Confidence

    b. Health

    c. Family

    d. Home

Conclusion

To quote my oldest son Simon, "Superheroes aren't real." Despite the messaging that tries to convince us that we have to be perfect—flawless, inexhaustible, giving to everyone but ourselves—the truest version of ourselves is whatever makes us feel confident, beautiful, and healthy.

We are much more than the toxic mindset telling us we'll never be enough. Scores of women are working to become their best selves right now, and social sellers are working to support them. You can stand alongside these women by investing in yourself while helping your friends achieve their goals.

Shopping social supports real people: neighbors, friends, family. It allows us to invest our most valued and limited resources, our time, our energy, and our money, into people we care about, instead of corporations and retailers that don't know us.

As you've been reading this book, I hope you've reached out to people to join your circle. Take that first step, like I did, of intentionally deciding what you need, then look for the right people to assist you in each area of your life. Who can you look to for advice on your health and your home environment, and on specialized topics like supplementation, skincare, and haircare? Start building your own micro-community of expert women and create your own circle.

I wish I had started sooner. It wasn't until February 2021 that I decided to go all in on building my circle of people who could help me live my best life. I began by building around my routines—those things I do on a regular, often daily, basis.

Most mornings, I have a shake for breakfast. It's quick, easy, and provides all the nutrients I need to start my day. I've figured out which supplements I need, and I take those each day as well. My skincare, makeup, and haircare routines are streamlined, effective, and efficient, and they all depend on the right products—moisturizer, toner, body lotions, and so on that deliver the results I want. I developed these routines with the help of my circle, and I know I can depend on them to get me whatever I need, when I need it.

Many of the clothes I wear each day come from my circle, and I have a regular workout routine that includes a coach from my circle and sports nutrition to provide energy and build muscle from another person within my circle. My essential oils, which I use for focus or to boost my immunity, come from someone in my circle. Likewise, my household products, such as cleaners and room fresheners, come from people I trust in my circle.

I have a nightly skincare and supplement routine, too, and I developed these—surprise—with help from my circle. I don't just buy products and start routines without giving them a lot of thought. I'm intentional about the problems I want to solve, the goals I want to achieve, and the woman I want to be. I seek help from people who are knowledgeable in each area of my life. I look at the testimonials they've received from other people who shop social, and I try the products, programs, and routines they offer. They don't always work out perfectly for me, but I know purchasing from my circle means there's no risk. I can talk to them about what I liked or didn't like about the product, and they're always there to help me find what I need to live my best life.

On my shopping social journey, I've also found authors and books I believe are in line with my thinking. They helped me on my path to becoming a better version of myself, so I hope you'll indulge me as I recap the lessons here and provide recommendations for further reading.

Intentionality

No matter where you are right now, you have the power to create a better life. It all starts with getting clarity around what you want and being intentional about how to get there.

When you're figuring out the next steps to take, Tom Paterson's LifePlan process and his book, *Living the Life You Were Meant to Live*,[4] are great resources. When I shifted from the corporate world into full-blown entrepreneurship, I had my LifePlan facilitated through the Paterson Process. It helped me gain clarity about who I am and what I can contribute to the world so I could take steps that eventually changed my life. I'm grateful for this experience, and because of it I now help other people go through this process as a LifePlan facilitator.

Knowing You, Growing You

You have so much to offer the world, and you deserve to be seen. The only thing holding you back is you. Confidence is within your reach, and simple external changes, such as a new haircut, can help you internalize your power. It's time to invest in yourself because you're worth it.

If you're looking for a confidence boost, I highly recommend my friend Lydia Fenet's book *The Most Powerful Woman in the Room is You*.[5] Not only is the book a fun read, but it has taken me to a new level of walking in my confidence, owning who I am, and articulating this boldness in my work and life.

---

[4] Tom Paterson, *Living the Life You Were Meant to Live*.

[5] Lydia Fenet, *The Most Powerful Woman in the Room Is You: Command an Audience and Sell Your Way to Success* (New York: Gallery, 2019).

Healthy You

Break free from the old lies and toxic mindsets that prevent you from reaching your true health. If you can't prioritize your health, then all of the changes you want to experience will be difficult—or impossible. Connecting with the right products, services, and habits will help you reach your health goals.

Healthy Family

If you're a parent, it's your responsibility to lead by example and teach your kids how to build good habits and mindsets that will keep them from falling into the struggles you've experienced. It will take time to reach true health for your family, but with flexibility and perseverance you can find what works for the people who matter most.

Healthy Home

You spend a lot of time in your home, and you deserve a healthy, restful retreat. By making conscious decisions about what goes into your home, you can find the right products and create a space that aligns with your vision of true health.

What If I Fail?

Don't let your fear of failure hold you back. Accept that failure is a part of the process, and what matters most to your success is how you react to failure. Not everything is going to work out, but what's important is that you keep trying. Others might try to discourage you, but you can stay solid in your truth and do what's best for you and your family.

Two books that helped me grow and gain perspective on my life are Henry Cloud's *Safe People*[6] and *Changes that Heal*.[7] They helped me learn how to become more vulnerable, which is essential for facing failure, and they also helped me recognize which people are in my court and which people aren't.

I am very hard on myself, and I recognize that a lot of other women are too. If you struggle with giving yourself grace, Aundi Kolber's *Try Softer*[8] is a good place to start.

Real Results

Finding the right routine takes time and intentionality, but if you go through the process, you'll find real results that make the effort well worth it. To experience long-term results, you have to make a

---

[6] Henry Cloud and John Townsend, Safe People: How to Find Relationships That Are Good for You and Avoid Those That Aren't (Grand Rapids: Zondervan, 1995).

[7] Henry Cloud, Changes That Heal: Four Practical Steps to a Happier, Healthier You (Grand Rapids: Zondervan, 2018).

[8] Aundi Kolber, Try Softer: A Fresh Approach to Move Us out of Anxiety, Stress, and Survival Mode—and into a Life of Connection and Joy (Carol Stream: Tyndale, 2020).

long-term investment. Figure out how to reach real results by grounding your habits in your physical, intellectual, emotional, and spiritual being.

For readers who want to go more in depth with the replenishment and energy management that I use in my LifePlan facilitation for clients, turn to Jim Loehr's *The Power of Full Engagement*.[9]

Supporting Your Friends Through Shopping Social

Shopping social supports your friends and connects you to like-minded, growth-focused people who truly care about you. When you're intentional about what you need and whom you support, you'll experience growth beyond what you could have imagined.

I would say I can't imagine where I would be today if I hadn't made the intentional choice to become a social shopper, but I actually can. I would be stuck in the same place where I was years ago: unhappy, unfulfilled, seeking the changes I didn't know were possible. I wouldn't have the support I have today—a circle of incredible women who have helped me through some of the darkest times in my life. Instead, I am full of life. By investing in myself, my family and friends have also benefitted, and I'm able to give much more to those around me without feeling empty and exhausted. I am so thankful for this wonderful journey that has changed my life.

---

[9] Jim Loehr and Tony Schwartz, The Power of Full Engagement.

I invite you to share your own journey with me and join a community of encouraging, growth-minded women. I believe in you, and I'm so proud of how far you have come.

* * *

If you've enjoyed this book,
I hope you'll leave an Amazon review
and connect with me at danaroefer.com,
on Instagram @danaroefer, and on LinkedIn at /danaroefer.
And remember to #shopsocial.

Acknowledgments

I'm inspired by the women who are doing this work. They are betting on themselves to help their clients improve their lives, while they build a better future for themselves and their families. They invest in themselves and inspire me to invest even more in myself. If you are one of these women, I see you, and I acknowledge what you're doing is hard. Remember that it's valuable, *especially* when it's hard.

I'm grateful for this industry that has allowed these women who might otherwise not have had the opportunity to become entrepreneurs to take charge of their destinies and make positive contributions to their friends, families, and communities.

Above all, I'm thankful for a life of surrender to Jesus and where He has led me. I will spend all of my days seeking to be fully all that He has created me to be. And for my husband Matt, my boys, and my parents for encouraging me to create this beautiful life full of joy and hope, even when things are hard. Especially when they're hard.

About the Author

DANA ROEFER is a social selling corporate consultant and LifePlan facilitator who is on a mission to help women recognize their worth, live with intentionality, and transform their buying habits. An active social shopper, she believes that building a microcommunity of experts with a vested interest in your well-being is the key to optimal, focused investing in yourself, your home, and your family. Dana is an advocate for entrepreneurship and supports women who have found financial independence and personal and professional fulfillment through starting their own businesses. She is dedicated to showing potential social shoppers how they can change their lives by relying on their circle of entrepreneurs—their social sellers.